BLUE JAYS
TRIVIA QUIZ BOOK

BOB ELLIOTT

McClelland & Stewart Inc.
Toronto, Ontario

The Toronto Sun Publishing Corp.
Toronto, Ontario

Copyright © 1993 by McClelland & Stewart Inc. and The Toronto Sun Publishing Corp.

All rights reserved. The use of any part of this publication reproduced, transmitted in any form or by any means, electronic, mechanical, photocopying, recording, or otherwise, or stored in a retrieval system, without the prior written consent of the publisher – or, in case of photocopying or other reprographic copying, a licence from Canadian Reprography Collective – is an infringement of the copyright law.

Canadian Cataloguing in Publication Data

Elliott, Bob, 1949-
Blue Jays trivia quiz book

Co-published by: Toronto sun.
ISBN 0-7710-8554-0

1. Toronto Blue Jays (Baseball team) - Miscellanea.
I. Title.

GV875.T6E55 1993   796.357′64′09713541   C93-093458-X

Cover photograph by Norm Betts/Toronto Sun
Text design by Nargis Churchill
Edited by Glenn Garnett/Canada Wide Feature Service Ltd.

Toronto Blue Jays and the Blue Jays' Logos are registered trademarks of Toronto Blue Jays Baseball Club. All rights reserved.

Printed and bound in Canada

McClelland & Stewart Inc.
The Canadian Publishers
481 University Avenue
Toronto, Ontario
M5G 2E9

The Toronto Sun
333 King Street East
Toronto, Ontario
M5A 3X5

CONTENTS

◆ Chapter One: Go Leafs Go	9
◆ Chapter Two: The Toronto Giants	23
◆ Chapter Three: Game One	39
◆ Chapter Four: The Expansion Blues	53
◆ Chapter Five: The Mistake by the Lake	67
◆ Chapter Six: Ode to the Blow Jays	81
◆ Chapter Seven: The Front Office	93
◆ Chapter Eight: Strange Days, Strange Jays	111
◆ Chapter Nine: The Best (and Worst) of the Jays	123
◆ Answers to Trivia Questions	137

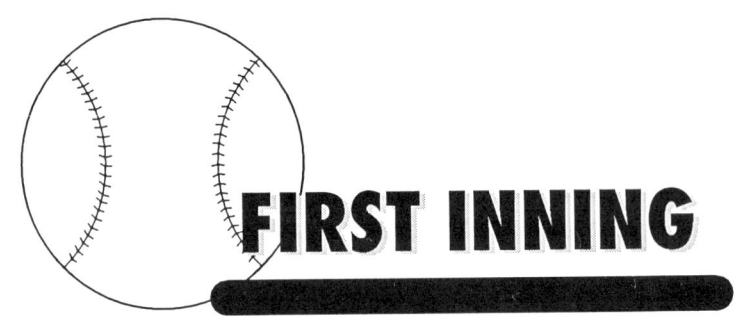

FIRST INNING

♦1. The cities of Seattle and Toronto were each granted American League expansion franchises in 1976. Which franchise was first?

♦2. In the expansion draft, the Mariners and Blue Jays were each allowed to select 30 players from existing clubs. How much did the teams pay for each player?

♦3. What was the official name of Toronto's expansion franchise before it became Toronto Blue Jays Baseball?

♦4. Toronto's 'name the team' contest drew more than 30,000 entries, of which 154 chose 'Blue Jays.' How was the winner selected?

♦5. During the summer of 1976, the New York *Times* reported a rumor that Toronto's major league baseball franchise was going to be moved to the National League, with an NL franchise taking its place in the American League. Name the team.

♦6. The Jays VP Pat Gillick played five years of pro ball, rising to Triple-A in the Baltimore Orioles chain. What position did he play?

♦7. What city by-law had to be amended before the Blue Jays could play ball at Exhibition Stadium?

◆8. Roy Hartsfield was appointed the Jays' first manager on September 21, 1976. But he had been in Toronto before, as a professional baseball player, during the early fifties. Name the team he played for then.

◆9. The Jays' first pitching coach was Bob Miller, who had first-hand knowledge of the joys and sorrows of playing for an expansion team — he was a member of the 1961 New York Mets. What was his claim to fame with that team?

◆10. The Jays' first batting instructor was a Red Sox great — name him.

◆11. Who was the first player acquired by the Toronto Blue Jays?

◆12. In the 1976 expansion draft, the Jays and Mariners were faced with slim pickings. Their AL brothers didn't have to protect players with less than three years of pro experience while 10 and 5 players (ten years of major league experience, with at least five years with the same club) were practically exempt. How many players were each of the existing AL clubs allowed to protect?

◆13. The Toronto Blue Jays picked second in the 1976 expansion draft and selected SS Bob Bailor from the Orioles. The Mariners had the first selection — whom did they choose?

◆14. The Jays were very fortunate to pry shortstop Bob Bailor away from the Orioles; but with a Gold Glove shortstop already in the Orioles lineup, there was no room for Bailor. Name the shortstop.

◆15. The Jays picked up Jim Mason from the New York Yankees in the '76 expansion draft. What was Mason's claim to fame with the Yankees during the '76 World Series?

◆16. Why did the Orioles leave an excellent prospect like Bob Bailor unprotected in the '76 draft?

◆17. What do the following major league players have in common: Elrod Hendricks, Sandy Alomar Sr., Lou Piniella, Boog Powell and Rico Petrocelli?

◆18. Shortly after the expansion draft, the Jays made their first trade, moving pitcher Al Fitzmorris to the Indians for IF/OF Doug Howard and another player — name him.

◆19. What was the average player salary on the Jays' major league roster in their opening season?

◆20. Tom Cheek has been the commentator for virtually every game the Jays have played since their inception, most of them with sidekick Jerry Howarth. But in 1977, Tom Cheek shared the broadcast booth with a former Cy Young Award winner. Name him.

◆21. During the expansion draft, Seattle wanted the order of selection kept a secret, with the names released later in alphabetical order. Why?

◆22. Rico Carty was drafted from the Cleveland Indians but was immediately traded back for John Lowenstein and a catcher. Name him.

◆23. This original Jay was runner-up AL Rookie of the Year to Al Bumbry in 1973. Name him.

◆24. This Jays coach was the last manager of the International League's Toronto Maple Leaf franchise before it closed in 1967. Name him.

◆25. This player was traded to both Canadian major league franchises in their first years of operation. Name him.

◆26. This Blue Jay pitcher was an Ontario Senior Inter-County League all-star in 1971. Name him.

◆27. Bobby Cox played briefly for the New York Yankees in the late sixties. What position did he play?

◆28. Which Blue Jays coach was involved in the biggest baseball trade of all time?

Answers begin on page 137.

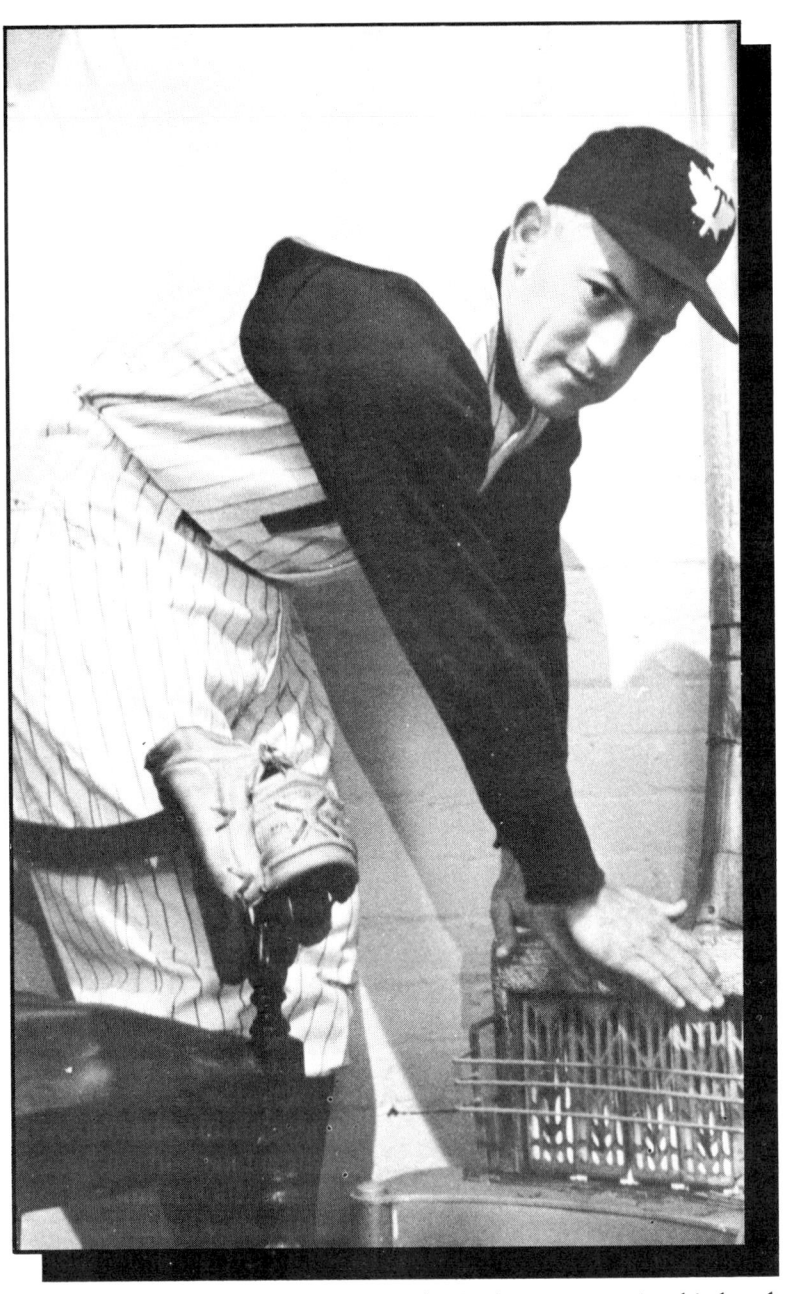

That's Maple Leafs manager Sparky Anderson, warming his hands by a heater at Maple Leaf Stadium on Opening Day 1964.
photo: Toronto Sun Archives

GO LEAFS GO

CHAPTER ONE

What is the most storied name in Canadian sports history?

Les Canadiens, of course, with all their Stanley Cup championships.

But *after* the Habs, the most respected franchise in Canada would be the Toronto Maple Leafs. Remember Johnny Bower, Terry Sawchuck, Red Kelly, George Armstrong, Dave Keon, Punch Imlach and all those other hockey pucks?

Well, it turns out the original Maple Leafs weren't hockey players worried about things like four-pointers and empty-netters.

Turns out the Toronto Baseball Club in the International League assumed the nickname of the Maple Leafs as early as 1903. Not until February 14, 1927 did Conn Smythe change the name of his hockey club from the Toronto St. Patrick's to the Toronto Maple Leafs.

The first game the Toronto baseball franchise ever played was May 22, 1886, when the Torontos beat Rochester by a 10-3 score at The Park Over the Don, which was long before Dave Stieb had become a cranky gleam in his grandparents' eyes. It was the first of many victories for the Torontos, who would become the Maple Leafs two decades later.

In all, Toronto won 15 International League Triple-A championships, including three triumphs in the Governor's

Cup (emblematic of the league championships). They started off with a five-year pattern, winning every half-decade: 1897-1902-1907-1912 and 1917 before repeating in 1918.

When the Leafs ceased to exist and the franchise was sold in 1967, they had been the oldest continuous members of the International League, a 78-year operation.

Many famous, and even more not-so-famous players, stopped off in Toronto on their way up to the majors. Or on the return trip down. Two of the more successful were managers, Dick Williams and Sparky Anderson. Each made the transition from player to manager, with Maple Leaf Stadium serving as the launching pad for careers managing major league dynasties.

"I was well groomed on fundamentals from my days with the Dodgers," says Williams, "but those first years in Toronto set forth my whole career."

Williams managed the Leafs, then the affiliate of the Boston Red Sox, to a third-place finish in 1965 and a second-place finish in 1966. Both years he was at the controls as the Leafs won the Governor's Cup, beating Columbus in 1965 and Richmond in 1966. The next year he brought home the Red Sox — 100-to-1 longshots — to a World Series berth. The St. Louis Cardinals were victorious in seven games over a Boston team Maple Leaf fans could identify with. Many of the players had helped Williams in the International League and in that 1967 World Series, they came one game short in pulling off the Impossible Dream.

They drove in runs, they pitched big games and they made all the plays with the glove: Reggie Smith, who led the American League the next year with a .320 average; third baseman Joe Foy, who won AL Rookie of The Year honors in 1965; second baseman Mike Andrews, reliever Galen Cisco (yes, the Cisco kid who now serves as pitching coach of the Blue Jays), catcher Russ Gibson, reliever Billy Rohr, catcher Mike Ryan and right-hander Gary Waslewski.

Waslewski almost didn't make it to Boston. He'd been traded in 1966 to the Kansas City organization for lefty reliever Guido Grilli.

"Gary was driving to Vancouver where their club was," recalls Williams from his Las Vegas home. "But it turned out Grilli wouldn't be able to report for five days so we cancelled the trade. We got that done, that wasn't a problem. Finding Gary who was already on his way wasn't so easy."

The Leafs asked the Ontario Provincial Police to track down Waslewski, who was driving west with his girlfriend. The OPP did get their man. He returned to Toronto and "wound up winning 18 games for us," said Williams. "The next year I used him to start Game Six of the World Series."

From Boston, Williams moved on to Oakland where he won three straight AL pennants, then on to California to manage the Angels. Next came the Montreal Expos, San Diego Padres — another trip to the World Series — and finally the Seattle Mariners.

In the Jack Kent Cooke era, the Maple Leafs won the championship in 1954, finished second by half a game in 1955, won again in 1956 and 1957. Just like Williams did in his years. The difference was while Cooke was drawing 446,040 fans to earn him Minor League Executive of the Year award from *The Sporting News* in 1952, attendance shrunk to under 100,000 in 1966 under Bob Hunter, who ran the community-owned club.

"I remember coming into Toronto in 1953 when I was playing for the Montreal Royals and Maple Leaf Stadium was sold out," says Williams. "Every time the Leafs scored a run they fired off a cannon. The two years I managed they only repainted the lower portion of the grandstand because we drew less than 1,000 fans per game. And there weren't any cannons being fired when we scored. The club couldn't afford it."

How bad was it?

"It was so bad that when we won the whole thing on the road in Richmond in 1966, the club couldn't even afford to buy the players champagne. A writer went out and bought champagne. The Red Sox reimbursed him later."

Williams' successor was a man named George Anderson, who played second base in a Maple Leaf uniform beginning in 1960. In 1964, Anderson, or Sparky as everyone called him, took over as manager.

"Everyone on the team was older than Sparky," recalls Williams. Anderson was grey by 30 years of age when he took to the manager's office for the first time.

"How could they put such an old head on such a young body?" jokes Anderson. Before the season started, he predicted the Leafs would finish first or second.

"I was a rash young rookie who thought he knew everything about this game," says Anderson, looking back on his first year. "In the first two months I got a real education. I discovered that matching teams on paper could drive a guy to cutting out paper dolls. You don't take into account things like injuries, bad breaks, errors, umpires or a dozen other items that can cost a ball club."

How frustrating was his first year?

"There were times a player who hadn't hit three home runs in two years beats you with a blast in the final inning," said Anderson. "Or our pitcher makes a real good pitch and the guy belts it out of the park. Who do you blame?"

Anderson's Leafs finished fifth. Five seasons later Anderson was in Cincinnati managing the Reds. His Big Red Machine won the NL West Division four of the next six years and won back-to-back World Series championships in 1975 and 1976. In 1979 he took over the Detroit Tigers where he nightly watches his bevy of home run hitters try to hit the ball all the way back to Ontario.

Few Leaf fans could envision Anderson going on to the success he enjoyed. Williams was a different matter. His clubs played to a level above their abilities. It was a trait all his clubs had.

"It was the same all year," said Williams when the Leafs beat Columbus in 1965. "We had no power hitters, no standout fielders. Everyone did their job."

While Williams was living the "Impossible Dream" in 1967, the Maple Leafs were noticing the light at the end of the tunnel. It was a freight train loaded with bill collectors.

In their final season a grand total of 67,216 paying customers showed up to watch the sixth place team. The franchise and its debts were sold to Louisville. Professional baseball didn't return until 1976 when Toronto was granted an American League expansion franchise.

Still, it was a grand journey the Torontos and then the Maple Leafs provided summer after summer, from Diamond

Park, to Hanlan's Point in the Toronto islands on Lake Ontario, to Maple Leaf Park and finally Maple Leaf Stadium on Fleet Street. The memories are plentiful, and they are all in Lou Cauz's excellent historical perspective on the Maple Leafs franchise entitled *Baseball's Back in Town.*

From lyrical, memory-provoking, unforgettable baseball names like Ned (Cannonball) Crane, Yencer Widensaul, Urban Shocker, Peaches Graham and Johnny Lush to Red Wingo, Murph Blandford, Lanky Joe Mulligan, Emory (Bubba) Church and Lu Blue.

From George (Twinkletoes) Selkirk, Luke (Hot Potato) Hamilton, Lena Blackburne, Joe Altobelli and Sam Jethroe to Stubby Overmire, Chi Chi Olivo, Joe Amalfitano, Mel McGaha and Pat Scantlebury.

From the tripleheader the Torontos lost in 1896; to the winner's share of the 1907 post-season gate ($692.92 per player); to fans taking the ferryboats to the Island to see Baldy Rudolph roll off 18, 23, 23, 18 and 25-win seasons from 1908 until 1912; and to the first professional home run of a young Providence slugger named Babe Ruth on September 5, 1914 at Hanlan's Point off Toronto pitcher Ellis Johnson.

From Elston Howard winning MVP honors in 1954; to Loren Babe starting a triple play in 1956; to Rocky Nelson's strange batting stance in 1958; to televised games during the 1961 season and finally to a 7-2 Syracuse win in front of 802 fans September 4, 1967 in the final game the Maple Leafs ever played.

Neil MacCarl, the dean of Canadian baseball writers, covered the Leafs for 19 years for the Toronto *Star.*

"The 1960 Maple Leafs might have been the best team," recalls MacCarl. "They won 100 games, 32 by shutouts."

Best game he ever saw?

"That same year Al Cicotte pitched an 11-inning, no-hitter to beat Montreal 1-0 and clinch the pennant," said MacCarl. "Bill Kunkel (later an AL ump) started for the Royals."

Which player's talents did MacCarl appreciate the most? Elston Howard, who went on to star with the Yankees? Reggie Smith, who did the same with the Red Sox? Sam

Jethro, Bobby Tiefenauer or Archie Wilson maybe?

Nope.

"Lew Morton from Ada, Oklahoma," says MacCarl. "He played about eight years."

Only Mike Goliat had more career at-bats than Morton — seven more. The outfielder had a career average of .273 and hit 120 homers.

"They had a night for him once and raised $380," said MacCarl. "After the game they presented him the cash. He turned around and presented it to the North Toronto Little League because his son had played there that summer and because that's the type of guy he was."

Like the Blue Jays, the Leafs had their legions of fans. In both cases Harvey Trivett was there early and stayed late following the fortunes of both teams.

"The best Maple Leaf player I ever saw was Bob Elliott (no relation to the author)," said Trivett, now president of the Blue Jays fan club. Elliott led the Maple Leafs with a .328 average in 1939. In 1947 he won the National League's Most Valuable Player trophy while with the Milwaukee Braves, the last NL third baseman to win the award until Philadelphia's Mike Schmidt won it in 1980.

Over the years the Maple Leafs had the best young players from many organizations. Besides having a working agreement with the Boston Red Sox, the Detroit Tigers, the Philadelphia Phillies, Pittsburgh Pirates, St. Louis Browns, Milwaukee Braves, Washington Senators and Cleveland Indians all sent farmhands to Toronto at various times.

The road to Cooperstown covers many a diamond and no less than 12 spent time in Hogtown.

In 1898, slugging first baseman Dan Brouthers batted .333 for the Torontos. He was elected to the Hall of Fame in 1945 after 14 .300-plus seasons.

Edward Grant Barrow arrived in Toronto at the turn of the century. He purchased a portion of the team and managed it to a championship in 1902. He later joined the Red Sox as manager in 1918 and little by little gave left-handed pitcher Babe Ruth more and more playing time in the outfield. Two years later Ruth was sold to the Yankees, Barrow became the Yankee GM and Ruth made the transformation into an everyday outfielder. With Ruth in right field the Yankees were on their way to 14 AL pennants and 10 World Series wins in a 26-year period. He was enshrined into the Hall in 1953.

In 1907, playing-manager Joseph Kelley took over the managing reins of the Maple Leafs. He turned a last-place team into league champs, beating Columbus of the American Association in the Junior World Series. After being drafted by Boston, Kelley was back in 1909 to manage and play centre field. The Leafs repeated in 1912 with a 91-win season. He managed so long (seven seasons) and so well the club was eventually known as 'The Kelleyites' before leaving after the 1914 season. His 567 wins are second on the all-time list of wins by Maple Leaf managers. Kelley was a career .317 hitter in the majors and played for five championship teams: the 1894-96 Baltimore Orioles and the 1899-1900 Brooklyn Superbas. Kelley was named to the Hall in 1971 by the Veteran's Committee.

Wee Willie Keeler of 'Hit 'Em Where They Aren't' fame arrived to play for the Leafs in 1911. He batted .278 for the third-place Leafs. The two-time NL batting champ, acclaimed by many as an expert bunter and the game's best 'place' hitter, was inducted into Cooperstown in 1939.

In 1917, playing-manager Larry (Nap) Lajoie took over and, at 41, brought a championship to Toronto. (That year a 13-year-old fan named Allan Lamport didn't have a nickel for the ferry to the island. So the future mayor of Toronto swam across to get to the game on time.) Lajoie slammed 221 hits in the 154-game schedule. After being the game's best second baseman, he moved to first and helped the Leafs win the title against Providence on the final day of the season. Three times an AL batting champ (twice with Cleveland and once with Philadelphia) he finished with 3,251 hits and was admitted to the Hall in 1937.

In 1920, Hugh Duffy managed the Maple Leafs to 108 wins. They finished with a .701 winning percentage *and* finished second. Duffy owned the highest single-season batting average ever, .438, with the Boston Red Sox. He tutored a lanky rookie outfielder with the Red Sox named Ted Williams. The Veteran's Committee elected Duffy in 1945.

Unlike Keeler and Lajoie, who were on the downside of their careers, second baseman Charlie Gehringer was 22 when he cleared customs. The youngster batted .325 with 25 homers and 108 RBIs. A player like that wasn't staying around Toronto long. For 17 years he played second base for the Tigers and won the MVP award in 1937 as old-timers compared his talents to Lajoie. He entered the Hall of Fame in 1949.

Lefty Carl Hubbell was another one on his way skyward when he arrived the next season. Again the Leafs were a farm team of the Detroit Tigers and orders from the corner of Michigan and Turbull were that Hubbell was not allowed to throw his screwball for fear of damaging his elbow. He compiled a 7-7 record and was far from owning ace-of-the-staff status. Years later the Tigers dealt him away and Hubbell reached the majors with the New York Giants. Twice he earned MVP honors, the only peace-time pitcher to do so. Winner of 253 games, Hubbell's greatest achievement came in the 1934 All-Star Game at the Polo Grounds. He struck out Babe Ruth, Lou Gehrig, Jimmie Foxx, Al Simmons and Bill Dickey in succession. Hubbell was inducted in 1947.

Heinie Manush arrived in T.O. for the 1938 season. He batted .310 as his career wound down. In 1926, after taking over for Ty Cobb in centre field for the Tigers, he went 6-for-9 in a doubleheader on the final day of the season to edge Babe Ruth for the batting title. After playing with the Browns, Senators, Red Sox, Dodgers and Pirates he was elected to the Hall by the Veteran's Committee in 1964.

In 1943, Ralph Kiner made Maple Leaf Stadium part of Kiner's Korner. The youngster was only in town for 41 games before signing on with the U.S. Navy. He managed two homers with the Leafs, but for seven years led the National League in homers, including a career best of 54. He was named by the Veteran's Committee in 1975.

Ex-Yankee great Tony Lazzeri tried his hand at managing the Leafs for part of the 1939 season and all of 1940. His Leafs were consistent, finishing dead last in both years. Seven times Lazzeri had 100 RBI seasons for the Yankees' famous Murderer's Row. In 1991 Lazzeri was inducted into the Hall of Fame.

Burleigh Grimes continued the long line of managers with impressive credentials when he took over in 1942. On Opening Day with his club down 9-4 to Jersey City, the Leafs rallied for a 10-9 victory. In 1943 Grimes managed the Leafs to their first pennant in 17 years with a 95-win season. Grimes was in charge in 1944 and returned under Jack Kent Cooke's regime to manage in 1952 and 1953. The last legal spitballer in the majors, Grimes won 270 games in his 19-year career and was elected to the Hall in 1964.

Whether it was Elston Howard or Bob Elliott, Rocky Nelson or Steve Demeter, Lew Morton or Reggie Smith, the fans have their favorites. These were the men who sowed the seeds which bore fruit years later as SkyDome turnstiles clicked for the four millionth time in 1990.

They shouldn't be ignored in Toronto's baseball history as fans continue to crowd the SkyDome.

Brand new Jays Ron Fairly, Alan Ashby and Rick Cerone introduce themselves to Toronto in a Bay Street parade on April 7, 1977.
photo: Norm Betts/Toronto Sun

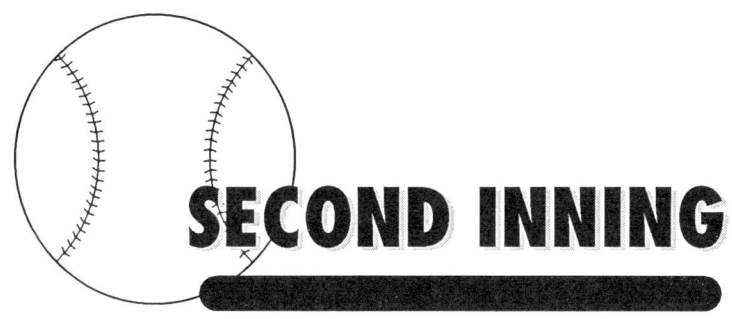

SECOND INNING

♦1. Everyone knows the Jays won their '77 opening game over the White Sox, 9-5. But did the Jays win their *very* first game, in spring training?

♦2. There were a lot more to follow, but this Jay was the team's very first contract holdout. Who was he?

♦3. This original Blue Jay batted right-handed for six years as a pro before becoming a switch-hitter, and discovered he hit better as a lefty. Name him.

♦4. Who threw out the ceremonial first pitch at the Jays' first game on April 7, 1977?

♦5. Two members of the White Sox playing the Blue Jays at the April 7, 1977 opener would later go on to join the team. Who were they?

♦6. Did the Jays win their second regular season game?

♦7. This Blue Jay was American League Player of the Month in the very first month of the team's existence. Name him.

♦8. One of the original Jays' oldest players, this 34-year-old middle reliever was the only pitcher in the majors to throw "an upshoot slider" and was known to throw underhand. Name him.

◆9. This original Jay was the only player in the majors in 1977 to throw left-handed but bat right exclusively. Name him.

◆10. On September 10, 1977, the Toronto Blue Jays blasted the New York Yankees 19-3, the most runs given up by the Bronx Bombers in half a century. Name the Jay who led the charge, who drove in a team-record nine runs on five hits, including two homers.

◆11. Jays pitcher Jerry Johnson, who picked up the franchise's first win, moved on to an unusual career once his playing days were through. What was it?

◆12. Who was the Blue Jays' first free agent signing?

◆13. Name the three Jays who made the Topps all-rookie team in 1977.

◆14. This versatile original Jay was a DH, pinch-hitter, IF, OF and catcher in his two terms with the Jays, before moving on to Japan. Name him.

◆15. An early *Sports Illustrated* article described the Toronto Blue Jays organization as "penurious," a term this first year Jay would no doubt use to describe the club after they turned down his request for a five-year, $60,000-a-year contract. In fact, he quit baseball — who was he?

◆16. What major league record did Blue Jay pitcher Dave Lemancyk tie with his win on the last day of the Jays' opening season?

◆17. Two long-time baseball veterans from the first-year Jays hung up their cleats after the '77 season — name them.

◆18. On November 17, 1977, the Jays participated in their first free agent draft. They were unable to sign their first selection, a common problem in the early years, because he wanted $3 million over five years. He went on to star elsewhere, before meeting a tragic end. Who was he?

◆19. What major league record did the Blue Jays' Ron Fairly share with Stan Musial?

◆20. Which Jay set the record for the highest batting average for a player on a first year ball club?

◆21. This Jays pitcher led the American League in pick-offs in 1977 — name him.

◆22. When asked for his assessment of the first year Jays, this seasoned member of the team said, "Doesn't matter how smart you are. In the history of the Kentucky Derby there's never been a mule even entered, let alone win the thing, so far as I know." Who said it?

Answers begin on page 141.

Herb Solway, Paul Godfrey and Don McDougall announce the purchase of the San Francisco Giants on January 9, 1976.
photo: Toronto Sun Archives

THE TORONTO GIANTS
CHAPTER TWO

Upon the demise of the Maple Leafs baseball club, one popular theory emerged as to what caused their departure into baseball's great beyond.

The most lasting impression was that super-salesman Jack Kent Cooke had sold baseball in the city of Toronto as it had never been sold before. Cooke tried hard for major league status before giving up on the International League Maple Leafs and heading to Los Angeles to start his own successful sports empire, which included the L.A. Lakers and Kings. The fans became so enthralled with what Cooke was selling, they took a look and discovered his International League product was minor league.

Cooke first mentioned those two little 'big' words — major league — to a city first beginning to spread its wings on to the world scene in 1951.

At one time or another Cooke attempted to buy the St. Louis Browns in 1953, who wound up in Baltimore; the Philadelphia Athletics, who moved on to Kansas City; and even the staid old Detroit Tigers, who simply stayed put. Cooke also applied unsuccessfully for an expansion team in the National League and was a founding father of the Continental League which was stillborn.

The problem for Cooke, as well as the sundry dream chasers who followed in the showman's footsteps, was the lack of a suitable stadium where baseball could be played in Toronto.

For years the discussion raged over a new ballpark. As early as 1954, Toronto Mayor Leslie H. Saunders said putting a new stadium on the site of the present Canadian National Exhibition would be "impractical since it couldn't be used for two weeks during the two weeks the Exhibition was held."

One dreamer named Paul Godfrey experienced baseball's chicken-and-egg theory regarding relocation/expansion first hand. As a North York alderman in 1969, he and then-mayor James Service tried to promote a domed stadium idea at the Downsview airport. The idea flopped because of cost.

"Mayor Service got me involved but a few months later he retired from office," says Godfrey. "That's when I picked up the ball. It disturbed me that Montreal was given a major league franchise. There hadn't been a champion of sports in Toronto since Allan Lamport was mayor and I made up my mind that now was the time to champion baseball for Toronto."

Lamport had repealed the bylaw which prevented Sunday sports being played in Toronto. While Lamport had battled a century-old city bylaw, Godfrey was moving into the holy catacombs of baseball's ivory towers.

He experienced a rude welcome when he attempted to move from the political world into the circles in which the lords of baseball move. At baseball's winter meetings in 1969 at the Americana Hotel in Bal Harbor, Fla., Godfrey jumped in front of commissioner Bowie Kuhn, blocking his path to speak to him for the first time. The conversation went something like this, after the introductions had been made:

Godfrey: "I'm from Toronto and we'd like to bring a ball team to our city."

Kuhn: "Where are you going to play?"

Godfrey: "Well, if you give us a franchise we'll certainly build a stadium."

Kuhn, placing his hand on Godfrey's shoulder: "Son, here's the way baseball works. You get a stadium to play in and then baseball will decide whether we'll come."

After that disappointing encounter, Godfrey's mission

was encapsulated by W.P. Kinsella's haunting line from *Shoeless Joe*: "Build it ... and they will come."

Four years later, baseball had grown and so had Godfrey on the Toronto political scene. He had graduated from North York alderman to Metro Toronto Chairman.

From 1969 until 1973, Godfrey attended major league baseball functions sporadically and for the next three years didn't miss an opportunity to be wherever owners gathered.

One turning point was the 1973 Grey Cup game at Exhibition Stadium between Edmonton Eskimos and the Ottawa Rough Riders. While waiting for the Governor-General to arrive, talk between Ontario Premier William Davis and Godfrey drifted to baseball and the chances of bringing a major-league team to town. A ball park remained the first hurdle to clear.

"But where can we put it?" asked the premier.

"Why not right here?" said Godfrey sweeping his hand out from the CNE grandstand. Godfrey pointed out where home plate would be and how the stadium could be used for both football and baseball. Godfrey said he thought he could get approval from Metro Council while Premier Davis said he'd take the matter to his cabinet.

With a stadium, or least the idea of a partial stadium solved, there still was the small matter of bringing a team to Toronto.

"I spent my time hanging out in hotel lobbies when I wasn't following owners into washrooms and restaurants, to sell them on the city of Toronto and the idea," says Godfrey.

While Godfrey was pushing the city up front, Don McDougall and Ed Bradley of Labatt's Breweries were sitting around talking how they could improve the market share of their product in the province of Ontario. At the time (1974) Molson's was No. 1 in Toronto, Carling was second and Labatt's third.

"Literally, the thought came while we were sitting around having a beer," recalls McDougall, then 38 and president of Labatt's. The Prince Edward Island native and University of Western Ontario graduate was trying to make inroads into Canada's richest province.

"We were involved in sponsoring golf and curling," says

McDougall, "but they didn't have the same local appeal in Toronto as hockey or football."

McDougall and Bradley thought: Why not major league baseball?

By then Premier Davis and Godfrey had announced plans to expand Exhibition Stadium to make it suitable for baseball. The province and Metro agreed to split the cost of refurbishing the stadium.

By that time Syd Cooper, of C.A. Pitts Engineering Construction Ltd., was already the first ambitious man out of the chute. He was heading a group seeking to bring a major league team to Toronto.

McDougall and his advisor Alan Eagleson — yes, the *same* Alan Eagleson — had a power lunch with Cooper and his group at the National Club in Toronto to see if Labatt's could get involved.

According to McDougall, the Cooper people told McDougall they weren't interested. The feeling among the Cooper group was that being associated with a beer company such as Labatt's "could adversely affect" their chances.

"I remember walking out the door with Alan and he said 'What about St. Louis? What about Milwaukee? What about Baltimore?' Those three teams were owned by breweries," says McDougall.

Just as he dominated Canada's participation in international hockey, Eagleson played a key role in the next move of the Labatt's group.

"Alan told us to just forget about trying to associate with groups and being part of a joint effort. He advised we should start out on our own," says McDougall. "He encouraged us not to depend on others but take the initiative."

From there the Labatt's group went to New York to talk to commissioner Kuhn, who told McDougall "baseball did not object to breweries being involved in baseball because they usually had deep pockets and showed good marketing sense.

"Kuhn said we should press on, but we should speak to the presidents of the respective leagues at the World Series," says McDougall.

While the Oakland Athletics and the Los Angeles

Dodgers were knocking heads by night in L.A.in the fall of 1974, three Toronto groups, each one making its own respective pitch, were taking their own swings in the afternoons. Lorne Duguid of Hiram Walker, representing Toronto Maple Leafs owner Harold Ballard, was the third party. Paul Godfrey was on hand, too, selling Toronto.

"By then it was a real dog and pony show," says McDougall. "Paul would go in and give a presentation why Toronto should have a major league team, then the Toronto groups would have their turns saying why they should own the team."

Besides the sales pitch, McDougall saw his first major-league game at the 1974 World Series. Not many exhibition games were played in P.E.I. "Didn't even know which team was from which league," jokes McDougall.

The same year, Labatt's met with a group interested in buying the Cleveland Indians and relocating in Toronto.

Selling the idea of purchasing a baseball team wasn't an immediate hit at Labatt's corporate offices. Molson's had sold Les Canadiens to the Bronfman brothers, Peter and Edward. "The feeling was that being involved in sports teams was a good promotion, but owning a team outright was not a smart business decision," McDougall says. "If the team did poorly the fans took it out on the owner or the owner's product. It was decided we would press ahead but we needed a partner."

Jake Moore, then chairman of John Labatt Ltd., suggested McDougall contact Page Wadsworth, chairman of the Canadian Imperial Bank of Commerce. Wadsworth thought Montreal financier R. Howard Webster, president of the *Globe and Mail*, owner of the Lord Simcoe Hotel and numerous other Toronto properties would be interested in getting involved. The three groups met in Wadsworth's office and a lasting partnership was formed. Labatt's and Webster would own 45 per cent each, while the CIBC, which would handle the financing, would take ownership of the remaining 10 per cent. Labatt's lawyer, Herb Solway, then introduced the group to Godfrey.

One month after the World Series was over, the group made a written offer to bring the Baltimore Orioles, for sale at the time, north. Three months later owner Jerold Hoffberger told the Toronto group he wouldn't be selling.

By that time, if you haven't guessed by now, frustration had set in. The group decided waiting for an expansion franchise would be hopeless and they continued to chase an existing team. Lawyer Herb Solway, acting for Labatt's, did the legal and logistical legwork which, he hoped, would bring Toronto its first major league team.

Solway set up an intricate network to let him know who was struggling and who wasn't and what teams were for sale. He was in early when Horace Stoneham attempted to sell the San Francisco Giants.

"It was common knowledge he was trying to sell," says Solway, downplaying his behind-the-scenes work. "If he had been able to find a buyer in San Francisco we wouldn't have even been involved."

Yet involved the Toronto group quickly became, even though other cities were looking for a team.

Solway made the initial contact with the Giants, talking with Don Christ, legal adviser to Giants owner Horace Stoneham and Jim Hunt, the Giants lawyer, in August of 1975. Stoneham, who had followed in the Dodgers' footsteps when they migrated west, was tired of drawing poor crowds in a wind tunnel known as Candlestick Park.

Now as the Toronto group prepared for another postseason trip, McDougall had lost his rookie status. Yet he wasn't quite a seasoned vet. A year after seeing his first major league game, McDougall told his secretary to make hotel reservations for the World Series.

"Where do you want to stay?" she asked.

"Why not stay the same place as last year?" answered McDougall matter-of-factly. In 1974, he'd been to Los Angeles to see Oakland. Someone else had to tell him the World Series moved around. And so it was to McDougall's surprise when he learned the Reds and the Red Sox would be playing in Cincinnati and Boston in the 1975 fall classic.

After lobbying feverishly and having meetings with Dodgers owner Walter O'Malley and National League officials, the group saw enough green lights to move on to the subject of greenbacks.

"Don McDougall and I met with O'Malley in his office overlooking Dodger Stadium," says Solway. "We were never aware of what he did behind the scenes but I had the feeling he was not overly helpful."

In November, the group made a formal offer of $12.5 million — $10 million of which would go to Stoneham and $2.5 million to cover damages for escaping the 17 years remaining on the Giants' lease at Candlestick Park.

Giants executive vice-president Charles Rupert and Hunt met Solway and McDougall at midnight, December 9 in Hollywood, Fla. They re-structured the offer and increased the total package. After four hours they were ready to draft an agreement. Now Stoneham would be paid $13.25 million — $8 million for the team and $5.25 million to cover litigation costs for the 17 years remaining on the lease.

"The league was worried about a lawsuit and we had looked into it," says Solway. "With the set figure of $5.25 million we were going to take out an insurance policy through Lloyd's of London to pay any damages. That way the company would defend the action."

Solway was told the Giants would have an answer to the Toronto offer Boxing Day. On December 28, both sides agreed subject to the approval of their respective boards. As a public company, the Giants couldn't be sold until the offer was presented at a board meeting.

On January 9, 1976 the Toronto group, with McDougall, Solway and Godfrey at the podium, announced they had an agreement in principal to buy the Giants for $13.25 million — roughly half of Joe Carter's latest contract.

The San Francisco Giants would soon have a new home in Toronto! Baseball would be back in town. Or so it seemed.

'Cross Your Fingers' is the way one headline greeted news of the conditional sale.

Even after reaching agreement with Stoneham, the Toronto group had to gain approval from nine of the 11 National League owners to be able to move the existing franchise and then hope that the city of San Francisco wouldn't object, that another buyer wouldn't surface, or that irate U.S. politicians wouldn't scream about the export of their national pastime during the bicentennial year.

"I didn't think we were home free," says Solway.

True, an immediate poll of the owners by Associated Press revealed only M. Donald Grant of the Mets and John Galbreath of the Pittsburgh Pirates openly opposed the sale. But while baseball fans in Metro rejoiced and talked of the tradition-rich team they'd soon call their own — names like Willie Mays, Willie McCovey, Bobby Thomson, John McGraw, former Maple Leaf Carl Hubbell, Mel Ott, Bill Terry and Christy Mathewson — people in high places, high on a hill in San Francisco, were fighting mad.

Right-hander John (The Count) Montefusco said if the club was sold he wouldn't report. While fanatics brushed up on the biographies of such non-household names as Dave Heaverlo, John D'Acquisto and Ed Halicki, the wheels were being put in motion to make sure the Giants didn't leave the city by the bay.

You know who won that battle and you know a group of American League castoffs came instead... but let's for a moment play What If?

What if the Giants had come to town, if the DH had stayed away — would baseball be as popular here as it is now?

Would the Toronto Giants and their fans have despised the Dodgers just as the old New York Giants hated 'dem Bums,' the Brooklyn Dodgers?

What would the over-and-under number be for the number of fights between fans when the Giants and the Expos played 18 times, nine games in Montreal and nine at Exhibition?

Toronto fans wouldn't have the Yankees to hate, you say? Well, New York, New York, the city so big they named it twice, according to philosopher/Baltimore Colts lineman Big Daddy Liscomb, had two teams. And the Mets of the eighties were far from lovable.

Rather than infielder Doug Rader, Toronto fans would have been cheering for catcher Dave Rader of the 1976 Giants.

Instead of having Willie Upshaw at first, they would have been able to witness the glove stylings and showmanship of Willie Montanez, acclaimed, at the time, the game's biggest hot dog before Rickey Henderson's arrival.

Rather than having Alfredo Griffin at shortstop, they would have spied Chris Speier, formerly of the Stratford Kraven Knits of the Inter-Country League, at short.

Derrel Thomas would have been at second, Steve Ontiveras at third.

In the outfield would have been Bobby Murcer, Von Joshua and Gary Matthews, not the Best Young Outfield in baseball, but at the time it was a lot better than what Toronto had.

The rotation would have consisted of John Montefusco, Jim Barr, Pete Falcone, Ed Halicki and Mike Caldwell. Gary Lavelle would be in the bullpen, well ahead of his arrival as a Blue Jay in the real world.

In the name of Bill Rigney, are we are getting ahead of ourselves! First, why didn't the Giants come to Exhibition Stadium after coming so close?

Well, when court opened in San Francisco Monday morning, January 11, city attorney Thomas O'Connor obtained a temporary restraining order against the Giants from moving. Newly elected mayor George Moscone took the hot potato and headed for Phoenix where the owners were meeting January 14, vowing to keep the Giants in San Francisco.

Thus began a long, torturous 29 days for the Toronto group.

The meetings in Phoenix came and went without a vote on the move to Toronto because of the restraining order.

On January 19, superior court judge John E. Benson postponed a hearing on an order restraining the sale of the club until February 3. On that date the Giants lawyers would have to show in court why the order should not be made permanent.

"There had to be signs of a local buyer for the judge to make the order permanent," says Solway. "Stoneham's lawyers had shown he would go broke. He couldn't allow that, not when there was an $8 million offer for the team."

Out of the bushes prospective buyers came, including one described in a San Francisco dispatch as 'multi-millionaire Bob Lurie, a local financier.'

On the eve of the hearing, an upset Giants lawyer Hunt

stated: "The city might as well ask the court to order San Franciscans to Candlestick Park and give them warm nights to enjoy the games," in an attempt to have the order dropped.

Hearing day came and went on February 3 as Judge Benson pulled a Judge Wapner and paused for a commercial. He put off making a decision on whether the Giants would be allowed to move. After hearing from both the city and the Giants lawyers, Benson headed to his chambers.

He'd barely closed the door when he heard a knock. It was shortstop Chris Speier. "He said he doesn't know when he'll make a decision," Speier said later. "I have to know if we're moving so I can look for a home in Toronto."

Two days later Bob Lurie, 46, said he was working on a syndicate to keep the Giants at Candlestick. The goal was $8 million. All the Lurie group had to do was match the Toronto offer for the sale of the club, since the $5.25 million of the purchase price was set aside for the litigation.

On February 10, the Toronto group was in New York answering questions from National League owners. That night Stoneham took McDougall and Solway to dinner at the famous restaurant, 21.

Meanwhile on the other coast, Judge Benson set D-Day for noon February 11 with spring training fast approaching on the horizon. In a seven-minute hearing, Benson told the city it had until high noon the next day to come up with an offer to match Toronto's bid. Mayor Moscone promised the money would be in place.

And on February 12, the headlines read: 'Toronto Has Struck Out.'

The Toronto Giants were 29-day wonders.

"The feeling was like letting a ground ball go through your legs," says Godfrey.

"That was what killed our chances," says McDougall.

Irish wakes have lasted longer than the city of Toronto's mourning period. Just 23 days later, the same Toronto group was granted an expansion franchise in the American League at meetings in New York. A few days later McDougall and the rest of the Toronto group signed the papers at the Host International Hotel in Tampa. Even securing the AL franchise didn't happen easily, but more on that later.

If the endless travel, the countless meetings and the constant spinning of his wheels weren't tough enough, Godfrey was assailed by Metro Toronto Council.

As far back as July of 1975, Toronto Aldermen Colin Vaughan and Michael Goldrick presented a motion of censure against Godfrey for spending $6,000 of the taxpayers' money on his mission to sell Major League Baseball on Toronto. Instead of censuring Godfrey, Metro Council — which had approved the spending before-hand — censured the two aldermen for their attack on the chairman.

Toronto Alderman Anne Johnston said Godfrey was wasting his time trying to land a major league team rather than working on Metro's budget. Toronto Alderman John Sewell mocked him for promoting the expansion of Exhibition Stadium to 55,000 seats.

"A lot of people ask me about trying to bring an NFL franchise to Toronto and ask 'How do you take all this?'" says Godfrey. "Well, this is nothing compared to the heat I took trying to bring Major League Baseball to Toronto. When the aldermen complained about spending $6,000, I told them how Mayor Jean Drapeau spent more on spilled champagne, bringing the Expos to Montreal."

Toronto baseball fans who waited breathlessly for the sale of the Giants in early 1976 could certainly relate to the situation Tampa Bay fans experienced last year. In the same scenario Tampa Bay thought it had purchased a ball club: newspapers ran supplements on the Tampa Bay Giants, T-shirts were sold and Will Clark posters were hung in youngsters' bedrooms.

Since the sale wasn't approved and local investors entered the picture at 11:59, the Tampa Bay Giants are only a memory of what might have been.

"It was deja vu," says McDougall, "the same thing for Tampa Bay and Toronto. Only the players were different."

Rico Carty clowns around during spring training in 1980.
photo: Norm Betts/Toronto Sun

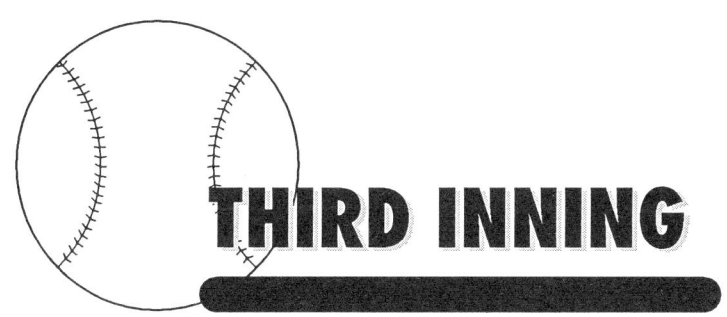

THIRD INNING

◆1. There was much outcry after the '77 season when the Jays traded their first relief specialist, Pete Vuckovich (7-7, 8 saves), with outfielder John Scott, to the Cardinals for Tom Underwood and another player, who would go on to become the Jays' best reliever of the early years. Name him.

◆2. On June 26, 1978, the Blue Jays defeated the Baltimore Orioles 24-10, the most number of runs the Jays have ever scored in a game. In this game, the youngest Blue Jay made his appearance, and it was an auspicious debut. Who was he?

◆3. DH Rico Carty was acquired three times by the Jays between 1976 and 1979, in three different ways. How?

◆4. In which batting category did Bob Bailor lead the American League in the '78 season?

◆5. Name the Blue Jay pitcher who was the Montreal Expos' first number one draft pick.

◆6. In the 1979 free agent draft, the Jays picked up future reliever Mark Eichhorn — but he wasn't a pitcher at the time. Name his position.

◆7. Sportswriters and fans were outraged when the Jays traded reliever Victor Cruz to Cleveland for rookie shortstop Alfredo Griffin and third baseman Phil Lansford. But the critics were silenced when Griffin's performance during the '79 season led to his selection as AL Rookie of the Year — an honor he shared with what other player?

♦8. In 1979, this Blue Jay outfielder became the first player in team history to play all 162 games. Name him.

♦9. After the Jays' dreadful 53-109 season in 1979, many were touting the "third year syndrome" as the reason for the franchise's backslide. Which team's third year futility mark did the Jays match?

♦10. Which two Jays' pitchers share the record for most credited losses in one season — 18?

♦11. When this outfielder was picked up in the June '79 free agent draft, Pat Gillick said he had the tools to be another Dwight Evans. Instead, he became a quarterback in the NFL — who is he?

♦12. After an 18-year-old ticket taker was fired from her job at Exhibition Stadium for "fraternizing with a player," this official upset the players when he told the press that he wouldn't want his daughter dating a Blue Jay. Who said it?

♦13. The 1979 Blue Jays were horrible, setting the "modern" record for finishing furthest behind the leader, at 50-1/2 games. But who were the all-time worst?

♦14. Admittedly, the Jays bullpen didn't get a lot of save opportunities during the '79 season, but in the end they set the major league record for the fewest saves ever. How many did they get?

♦15. Late in the 1979 season, the Jays called up 30-year-old pitcher Steve Luebber for a look. They didn't much like what they saw — in fact, he departed with the worst ERA in the history of the club. What was it?

◆16. What dubious record did shortstop Alfredo Griffin set in 1979?

◆17. What was the name of the exhibition series that pitted the Montreal Expos against the Toronto Blue Jays during the late seventies and early eighties?

◆18. In 1980, the Jays appointed Bobby Mattick as the team's second manager. Mattick's career as a player was hampered by a serious injury — what was it?

◆19. What two team rules did new manager Bobby Mattick rescind when he arrived in 1980?

◆20. What dubious record set by the Washington Senators in 1964 did the Jays barely avoid in 1980?

◆21. In November 1980, the Jays let this player get away to free agency when they signed Danny Ainge to a contract for the following year. The front office wasn't sorry to see him go — he served as the team's player rep and had a stormy relationship with management. Who was he?

◆22. The Philadelphia Phillies gambled and lost when they left this talented outfielder exposed in the December 1980 major league draft. The Jays scooped him up for only $25,000. Name him.

◆23. Bob Bailor was traded away in December 1980 to the Mets for this sweet-singing pitcher. Who was he?

◆24. In 1980, Danny Ainge received a $300,000 bonus from the Jays. What was it for?

Answers begin on page 143.

Alvis Woods trudges through the Opening Day snow with bats taped to his cleats on April 7, 1977. He later hit a homer.
photo: Julien LeBourdais/Toronto Sun Archives

GAME ONE
CHAPTER THREE

"*Baseball is North American culture. Cities that have major league teams are something. Those that don't are ... well, second drawer.*"

Toronto Sun editorial

When Major League Baseball finally arrived at Exhibition Stadium, home of the CFL's Toronto Argonauts, the day was less than top drawer. Starters lived up to expansion billing, errors were made and the weather was perfect.

Perfect *Grey Cup* weather!

Yet people who were there, and the number continues to grow each year, remember it simply as a wonderful afternoon.

Years down the road the memories of the first game the Toronto Blue Jays ever played will become as cloudy and snowy as your first old black-and-white picture tube on a bad day.

Even now, fact messes with fiction of the afternoon of that Thursday, April 7 debut at Exhibition Stadium in 1977, the day before Good Friday.

Before we get to the details, let's first try to separate fiction from fact.

Fiction: Groundskeepers cleared snowbanks from the carpet at Exhibition Stadium so the game could be played — the way you see snowplows do their work before NFL games. Later, during the game, players skirted snow drifts on their way around the bases.

Fact: Bob Bailor, the first player selected by the Blue Jays in the expansion draft, remembers roughly an inch of snow falling before game time.

Fiction: Line drives in the gap rolled towards the wall, causing a snowballing effect, the way cartoon characters are disposed of from mountain tops in a Bugs Bunny cartoon.

Fact: Peter Bavasi, president of the Jays at the time, has two Opening Day pictures taken from atop the Exhibition Stadium press box hanging in his Sportsticker offices in Jersey City, N.J. "The first picture was taken as the first pitch is thrown and the field is snow-covered," says Bavasi. "The second one was taken in the fourth and all the snow — except for a small area in right-centre field — had melted from the body heat of the crowd."

Fiction: Almost 200,000 fans jammed the tiny Ex, transformed from football stadium into a makeshift baseball park.

Fact: The turnstiles, those old ones in the 100-year-old football grandstand, and the brand new ones situated behind the new baseball grandstand, clicked 44,649 times on Opening Day as the Blue Jays defeated the Chicago White Sox 9-5 in their first game.

"When I'm in southern Ontario traveling on the winter caravan, it seems as if every other person I meet was at that first game," remembers Bailor, now the Jays first base coach. "By my count there must have been somewhere between eight and 10 million say they were there. I mean, every time I talk ball with someone in St. Catharines, or London, or Toronto, they were all at that first game."

Bailor, like the rest of the Jays, was assembled from the scrap heap of the existing 12 American League teams at the Plaza Hotel November 6, 1976. The expansion team gathered in Dunedin for workouts under rookie manager Roy Hartsfield.

On Monday, April 4, the lot left Florida with only eight wins in 24 games, led by the likes of outfielder Gary Woods (his 16 hits in Grapefruit League play were the most by any player) and outfielder Sam Ewing (who led the team in

Florida with four homers and 11 RBIs).

For the majority of Blue Jays, they would see their adopted home town for the next six months for the first time the next day.

"Sure beats anything they have back home in Verona," said Ewing, surveying the skyline. Ewing is a native of Verona, Tenn. which "has a population of 25, depending on who died, who was born and who left."

Bailor and Ewing toured the harborfront, city hall and the brand new Eaton Centre. A planned trip to the top of the CN Tower was canceled because of high winds. Bailor marveled at the Eaton Centre, but didn't know if showing his wife the place was a good idea, what with "all the expensive shops."

Ewing compared Toronto to San Francisco: "I like the idea of both subways and streetcars, both the old and the new."

Which is pretty much what the Jays were. Guys on the way down and peach-fuzzed youngsters trying the climb up the hill.

Looking head to Opening Day, forecaster Ed Roete of Environment Canada exhibited the same kind of hit-and-miss prognostication weathermen often show nowadays. "The weather isn't going to be terrific for baseball, but there will be no snow or rain."

Meanwhile, to the west, a Chicago forecaster predicted the White Sox would open the season "under light snow flurries."

Both the White Sox and the Blue Jays worked out on the Wednesday, April 6. Instead of the aroma of roasted peanuts, popcorn and hot dogs, the fresh smell of paint and still-drying plaster permeated the chilly surroundings. Tangled wires, hunks of wood, pails of paint and boxes littered the corridors at the new stadium.

Years from now people will tell their grandchildren about the first game the Blue Jays ever played. If you were there, you know all about it. If you weren't there, here are some finer points to help you convince even the most skeptical. It'll be our secret.

Light snow, roughly an inch, arrived before game time

as the temperature hovered below and above 0 degrees Celsius. "The snow was about as much as what you'd find on your windshield," remembers one worker. Groundskeepers manned the Zambonis to extract snow and freezing rain from the artificial turf in the infield.

"The snow on Opening Day was exactly what some southern players expected playing in Toronto to be like," says Bailor, who is no meteorologist. But coming from Connelsville, Pa., he knew better after a look at the map.

"I figured the weather in Toronto would almost be the same as what we had growing up in Pennsylvania. I knew you can have great weather in April or you have ... well, you can have the kind of Opening Day we had. Some players thought Toronto was located up around Hudson Bay or at least Georgian Bay, way up north. They thought we'd have snow all the time, a week of summer in July and after that it snow would start again."

Climate was the No. 1 question on the minds of the Jays leading up to the game and the season. And accurately so.

"The build-up to the first pitch on game day was like the build-up to the first pitch of the World Series," says Bailor, on the scene for both occasions in Blue Jays history.

Bailor had just returned from a hunting trip near his home when he was informed he'd been drafted by an organization called the Toronto Blue Jays. "I came in dirty from hunting, not really looking like a major leaguer. My father was excited, but he told me I'd been picked by Toronto. That was exciting! I asked him who else was on the team."

Well, there wasn't anyone else yet, besides catcher Phil Roof, purchased from Cleveland the night before the draft. Bailor was the first player drafted by the Blue Jays.

On the morning of April 7, there wasn't any doubt.

"Among the 50 players from the two teams there wasn't any doubt the game would be cancelled," Bailor remembers, "but on the other hand, there wasn't any doubt the game *would* be played on the part of Toronto management. We didn't realize the significance of the game until later.

"I mean, there will never ever be another 'first game' in the history of the Toronto Blue Jays," says Bailor.

Outfielder Alvis Woods taped a Louisville Slugger to

each foot and made like Jean-Claude Killy mushing across the snowy green carpet. All in good fun for Woods, who wasn't in the starting lineup.

Bavasi says if it had been Game Two, or Game 156, or any other game of the season it would have been cancelled.

"First thing we had to do when the umps got to the park was get them onside," says Bavasi. "Nestor Cylak, a great guy, was the crew chief, and he recognized the significance of playing. Plus with all the American writers in town to cover the game, it was appropriate we played. The stereotype of Canada at the time was Eskimos and ice floes.

"Our fans were a hearty lot. They weren't complaining."

Game One in franchise history began with right-hander Bill Singer, author of a no-hitter while a Dodger, on the mound for the Jays. Bavasi had grown up in the Dodger system and now he'd given the ball to a Dodger ex in an attempt to baptize a new franchise.

Pre-game ceremonies involving Premier Bill Davis, Metro Chairman Paul Godfrey and commissioner Bowie Kuhn had to be scrapped because of the snow. Songbird Anne Murray arrived in Bavasi's office to say her brothers had told her baseball wasn't like football and the show doesn't always go on if there is inclement weather. But Murray said "if you're still playing, I'll sing." Bundled in a red parka, Murray took to the cold to sing *O Canada* as the 48th Highlanders, wearing their customary kilts, stood in centre field.

Singer the pitcher, not Murray the singer, threw the first pitch of the afternoon — not a snowball, but a Rawlings ball autographed by Lee MacPhail, president of the American League — to White Sox lead-off hitter Ralph Garr.

"And," adds Bavasi, "presumably he threw his arm out on that first pitch."

Plate ump Chylak yelled out a spine-tingling "Steeee-RIKE."

Richie Zisk hit a two-run homer off Singer in the first and the metal benches down the line seemed even chillier on the backsides.

The day, when not dominated by the organist playing *Jingle Bells* and *Pennies from Heaven*, was to belong to a 27-

year-old Texan from Beaumont. While Sam Ewing had been the star of the Florida frolics, Jays first baseman Doug Ault homered in the first inning off right-hander Ken Brett, the older brother of eventual Hall of Famer George Brett, cutting the lead to 2-1. No one knew at the time, neither Ault nor the rest of the truly blue shivering birds, that it was only the first of two homers.

"The game shouldn't have been played from a player's point of view," remembers Brett, "but there were a lot of people there — a lot of them liquored up. If we hadn't have played the game the fans might have tore the stadium down."

In the second, the White Sox went ahead 4-1 on a run-scoring single by Allan Bannister and a double by Zisk.

Outfielder Gary Woods manufactured a run to cut Chicago's lead to 4-2 when he bunted for a base hit, stole second and scored on a single by second baseman Pedro Garcia, one of nine RBIs he would have that year.

Finally, Singer put a zero on the board in the top of the third and Ault brought the Jays even. While the first baseman had pulled an inside slider over the left-field fence for a solo homer in the first, he tagged another Brett slider for a two-run homer to right, tying the score at 4-4.

And like Singer, Brett was headed to the showers.

"The mound was slippery," Brett explains, "you had to shorten your stride. It was muddy and wet ... but it was also the same for both teams and they wound up beating the crap out of us.

"I made some bad starts over the years, I think the only thing I accomplished that day was to make a hero out of Doug Ault. Good for him, but it's a game I'd like to forget."

Ault had played with the Glacier Pilots of Anchorage Alaska, who won the U.S. National Baseball Congress championship in 1972, so Opening Day wasn't any shock to him.

"It's pretty cold up in Alaska in the month of June — no snow, but plenty of sleet," says Ault. "Another year when I was with Pittsfield we opened the season in Quebec City. Now *that* was cold."

Starting shortstop Hector Torres of Monterey, Mexico remembers telling someone on the bench how he'd seen snow before, but he could "never remember seeing 40,000 people sitting and cheering in the cold."

Second baseman Pedro Garcia doubled in the fourth and scored on a double by Dave McKay, which put the Jays ahead to stay as Brett was chased in the bottom half of the inning, just as Singer had departed in the top half, giving way to reliever Jerry Johnson.

Outfield Alvis Woods made the most of his pinch-hit-at-bat against Francisco Barrios in the fifth inning, becoming only the 41st major-leaguer to homer in his first at bat. Woods' two-run homer went over the right-field fence into what was left of the Argos' end zone.

Jays fans got their first taste of a nerve-wracking inning with a reliever on the mound in the eighth. Up 7-5, Pete Vuckovich struck out Eric Soderholm and Chet Lemon. But after getting two strikes on Brian Downing, who already had three hits in the game, Vuckovich issued a free pass. When Ralph Garr followed with a single, the tying run was on first and the lead run was striding toward the plate in the person of pinch-hitter Nyls Nyman. Nyman, however, flew out to centre fielder Gary Woods to end the inning.

In the bottom of the eighth, the Jays added some extra seat cushions for Vuckovich to ride home as Ault delivered a run-scoring single, and the ninth Toronto run scored when the White Sox turned a double play.

As is the tradition nowadays, fans left the park early, but this time there was good reason, with the wind, the cold and darkness approaching. Johnson pitched 2-2/3 innings for the first win in franchise history, but ended the sixth with the bases loaded and stranded two runners in the seventh.

"I thought I was going to die when I took my jacket off and that cold hit me," said Johnson, a Miami native. "Usually I'm deer hunting in weather like this."

Wearing their bicentennial uniforms, the last-place White Sox of 1976 managed to somehow strand 19 base runners — one shy of what was then the AL record — and managed to start the 1977 season by shooting themselves in their collective frost-bitten feet.

Besides Garr being the first hitter, Johnson registering

the first win and Zisk collecting the first hit (not to mention homer) at Exhibition Stadium, Allen Abel, the brilliant columnist for the *Globe and Mail*, noted other firsts:

The first firecracker went off in the fifth inning, shortly after the first roll of toilet paper unfurled itself from the centre field stands; the first bulb burnt out in the scoreboard in the eighth; the first tow truck arrived in the overcrowded parking lot at 3:30; Blue Jay Steve Bowling was the first to hit a fan in the head with a foul ball; the first chant of "We Want Beer" could be heard from the $2 seats in the football grandstand during the first inning. When Oscar Gamble grounded out to end the game, the first chants of "We're No. 1, We're No. 1" were heard from the chilled spectators.

As for Brett, he wasn't around when the "We're No. 1" chants were heard. For only the second time in 184 major-league starts, he left the park before the game was over.

"I wasn't going to sit around and to top it off there wasn't any hot water in the clubhouse so I couldn't shower," says Brett, now a broadcaster with the Angels. "I couldn't catch a cab so I had to walk back to the hotel.

"Thank God that park is gone."

Unlike 1985, 1989, 1991 or 1992, when the Jays won to venture into post-season play, fans did not hit the streets to party. A post-game party organized by the Toronto Jaycees at the Hotel Toronto drew only 400 people rather than the expected turnout of 2,000.

The special drink of the night was a Blue Jay cocktail made of rum, vodka and blue curacao for $3.75 each.

After the final out, well, maybe *before* the final out, the management group which brought Major League Baseball to Toronto took time to celebrate. It had been quite a ride the past 15 months.

In March 1976, just 23 days after the Giants had been lost, both the American and National Leagues were fighting over the right to put an expansion franchise in Toronto.

"The city of Toronto and baseball was like someone getting married on the rebound, except this one worked," said Paul Godfrey, after the Jays won the World Series.

"All the time we spent at meetings, lobbying for a team and trying to focus on buying a National League club, Lee

MacPhail (the American League president) would tell us 'Don't be surprised if you wind up in our league.'"

It turned out MacPhail wasn't just making nice-nice with his diplomacy.

On March 20, 1976, MacPhail announced in New York that AL owners had voted unanimously to expand to Toronto for the 1977 season. Not to be outdone, Feeney said the NL would consider expansion as well and Toronto would be included. It also came to light that another Toronto group was bidding for an expansion franchise.

The second group, late starters in the sweepstakes, surfaced before the meetings at Tampa the next week. It was headed by Phil and Irving Granovsky, head of Atlantic Packaging and included Trevor Eyton, a partner in the law firm of Tory, Tory, Des Lauriers and Binnington; Fred McCutheon, vice-president of Loewen, Ondaatje, McCutheon and Co. stockbrokers; James Kay, president of Dylex, owner of Tip Top Tailors, Harry Rosen Tailors and Fairweather Co.

How did the Labatt's people respond?

Well, when they heard that MacPhail was flying into Toronto to meet with the Granovsky group March 22, it was the Labatt's group which announced to the city's three dailies that MacPhail was coming the next day. Not only that, they picked him up at the airport, drove him to his meeting with their rivals, waited for him and then entertained him for the remainder of the day.

On March 26, AL owners voted 11-1 to award the Toronto franchise to McDougall's group. Baltimore owner Jerold Hoffberger, owner of Carling National Breweries in the United States, cast the lone dissenting vote.

Three days later, needing unanimous approval, the NL met to vote on expansion. Commissioner Bowie Kuhn was being pressured to give Washington an expansion franchise. Because of its close proximity to Baltimore (30 miles, or 48 km), Washington couldn't be given an AL franchise. Kuhn suggested the NL take Washington and Toronto while the AL add Seattle and either New Orleans or Denver, both less than major players on the expansion scene at the time. Apparently, at high-level owners meetings the NL had laid claim to Toronto first and the NL was now asking the AL to respect the agreement.

"This was the least written-about meeting and most important of all," says McDougall. "The AL owners were prepared to go into Toronto but not until the NL said it wasn't."

After McDougall gave yet another presentation attempting to sell the NL owners on Toronto, the vote was taken. The owners voted 8-4 in favor of expansion to Toronto and Washington. However, since unanimous approval was required, a 15-minute break was called. Another vote was taken and this time it was 9-3, with St. Louis, Cincinnati and Philadelphia against expansion. Again, time out was called.

"Mr. August (Gussie) Busch (of the St. Louis Cardinals) was dead-set against expansion," remembers McDougall, "but during the break I leaned on him, beer man to beer man."

Another vote was taken and the owner of the Cardinals switched. Still, the count was only 10-2, with both Phillies' Ruly Carpenter (whose father had adopted the Blue Jay insignia for his team briefly in the 1940s) and Bob Howsam, of the Cincinnati Reds, refusing to budge. By now, recalls McDougall, "the temperature of the water was getting pretty hot." Atlanta's Ted Turner and Montreal's John McHale (Charles Bronfman badly wanted Toronto in the NL) cornered Howsam during one break.

Unable to reach unanimity, the NL voted 8-4 that it would be not be in the best interests of baseball for a unanimous vote to be needed.

Once again the Toronto group was in its customary situation of suspended animation. It was a win-win situation for the city of Toronto, but still McDougall thought they might "wait forever for the NL to make up its mind, plus we didn't want to offend our friends in the AL."

Godfrey remembers Kuhn telling him: "'Give me a couple of weeks and I'll work on the two votes.' Well they had the vote and the vote changed all right — from 10-2 to 7-5 in favor of expanding." The NL didn't expand until 1992 when they put teams in Miami and Denver.

Kuhn's push to place Toronto in the NL earned the commissioner boos on Opening Day, while AL president MacPhail was cheered heartily.

So you NL lovers can blame the management of the Reds and Phillies for Toronto winding up in the American League. On the other hand, you die-hard AL fans, who grew up worshipping the Yankees and Tigers, can extend a thank-you the next time you see Cincinnati or Philadelphia on the highlights.

"I think the team would have been a success attendance-wise no matter what league it was in," says Godfrey, "but there was certainly a lot more fun starting from scratch, losing 100 games, growing into a contender. In the NL we would have had a ready-made team."

While the Jays were 100-game losers, the ball club's image accomplished the goal McDougall had been seeking in 1974. While beer didn't arrive at Exhibition Stadium until 1982, by the end of 1979 Labatt's was No. 1 in market share in Ontario.

For the Blue Jays to attain the same goal in the American League it would take a few more years, because after the win on Opening Day there were only 53 more wins during the 1977 season.

And 107 losses.

FOURTH INNING

♦1. This future baseball broadcaster and original member of the Kansas City Royals was acquired by the Jays from KC before the '81 season. Name him.

♦2. On May 15, 1981, this Cleveland pitcher threw a perfect game against the Jays — who was he?

♦3. Jays' infielder Danny Ainge won this highly coveted award in 1981 — name it.

♦4. When this Blue Jay saw his salary climb to $800,000 in 1981, he was briefly the highest paid athlete in Canadian history, the first Jay to make that claim. Who was he?

♦5. What feat, unprecedented for a Blue Jay regular starting pitcher, did Dave Stieb pull off in the 1981 season?

♦6. Which NBA team drafted Danny Ainge, and in which round was he selected?

♦7. In September 1981, the Jays became the first major league team to sign a player from this Far East country — name it.

♦8. After the 1981 season, the Jays signed their first full-time batting instructor — name him.

♦9. Jays president Peter Bavasi surprised everyone with his announcement after the 1981 season that he was stepping down. Who replaced Bavasi as president of the baseball club in '82?

♦10. At the 1982 Blue Jays training camp, three of the players invited, Junior Moore, Ted Cox and Damaso Garcia, already had something more in common than the dream of making the team. To what Blue Jay record had each made a significant contribution?

♦11. The emergence of this young Jays infielder made it possible for the Jays to trade their number one longball hitter, John Mayberry, to the New York Yankees early into the 1982 season. Name him.

♦12. Ernie Whitt may have been the last original Jay to go, when he was traded to Atlanta after the 1989 season, but 1982 saw the departure of the last player from the Jays' *opening day lineup*. Who was he?

♦13. When the Jays picked up outfielder Leon Roberts from the Texas Rangers, he told the press: "Really, I'd rather be in Japan." They traded him away the following season for a home run hitter who, after four seasons with the Jays, headed for the Far East himself. Who was he?

♦14. During the 1982 season, which two Jays were dubbed 'The Flying Wallendas' by Boston sportswriters?

♦15. One of Bobby Cox's first innovations as the Jays' new skipper in 1982 was the use of the platoon system, to get the most out of the talent available to him. Iorg and Mulliniks were the platoon at third; Whitt and Martinez took turns as catcher; who was Jesse Barfield's platoon partner that season in right field?

◆16. One of the big trades after the 1982 season saw the Jays send their relief ace Dale Murray along with cash to the Yankees for Dave Collins, pitcher Morgan and a minor league prospect. Gillick picked the Yanks' pockets again — who was the prospect?

◆17. On August 24, 1983, this Orioles reliever picked three Blue Jays off base in the same inning. Who was he?

◆18. The Jays' DH corps in 1983 topped the American League with 34 homers and 113 RBIs. Name the two players responsible for those numbers.

◆19. Name the only Jay who was an original member of the Seattle Mariners in 1977.

◆20. For three seasons, between 1984 and 1986, third baseman Rance Mulliniks led the American League in what category?

Answers begin on page 146.

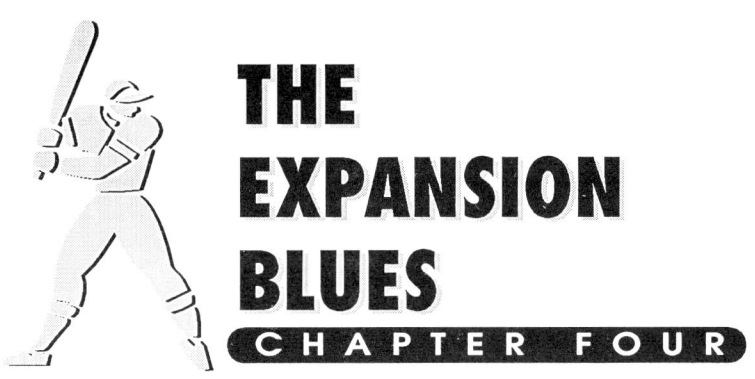

THE EXPANSION BLUES
CHAPTER FOUR

Their given name was the Toronto Blue Jays. For the first three years they were better known as the Toronto Expansion Blues.

Long before the arrival of a rotation dominated by Dave Stieb and Jim Clancy, before the Best Young Outfield in Baseball, the diving acrobatics of Robbie Alomar and the tape-measure shots of Joltin' Joe Carter, there were hard-working men like Bob Bailor, Tommy Underwood, Otto (the Swatto) Velez, Rick Bosetti and Balor Moore to cheer.

Yet for the most part, the main reason to go to Exhibition Stadium was to view the visiting nine. Established stars like Reggie Jackson, Rod Carew, Sparky Lyle, Jim Palmer, Jim (Catfish) Hunter and Jim Rice. They were more appealing and more talented than the castoffs and never-will-be's populating the Blue Jays' lineup.

Roy Hartsfield was the Jays' first manager, just as he was president Peter Bavasi's first manager. Bavasi, son of Buzzie Bavasi, one-time Dodger GM, entered the baseball world in 1964 as the business manager for Triple-A Albuquerque, where Hartsfield was managing the Dodgers' top farm club.

"I'd close the ticket booth as soon as I could, rush down under the stands to the clubhouse, come through the tunnel to the entrance of the dugout," remembers Bavasi. "Roy would let me stand there and listen to what went on during the games. I'd hear all of Roy's pearls of wisdom. Each night

Roy Hartsfield used "southern sayings" to get through to his battle-scarred charges, and equally colorful language with umpires.
photo: Mike Peake/Toronto Sun

I'd go back to my place and write them down on index cards. That's how I learned the game of baseball."

The 22-year-old young pup straight out of college and the veteran minor league manager swapped stories many a night. Eventually, Bavasi told his father, "You know, if I ever have the opportunity to run a ball club, Roy Hartsfield will be my manager."

Twelve years later, on June 18, 1976, it was officially announced that Bavasi had been hired as the executive vice-president and general manager of the Blue Jays. He wasn't long in phoning Hartsfield, who was managing Triple-A Hawaii in the Pacific Coast League and the call he placed to his second father wasn't just to shoot the breeze.

Hartsfield congratulated his friend of more than a decade, but couldn't believe the news when Bavasi told him he was going to be the first skipper of his expansion club.

"Peter was hired on a Friday, flew home to San Diego Saturday to see his father and Sunday morning, Father's Day, he woke Alice and I up at 8 in the morning to say I had the job," recalls Hartsfield. "He told me I would hear all kinds of names mentioned for the job — names like Elston Howard, Yogi Berra and Dick Williams — but I had to keep it a secret. He wanted the publicity surrounding the hunt for a manager."

Bavasi wanted to keep things quiet until after the World Series. The plan was to make the grand announcement of who would be the manager before the expansion draft.

"If Pat Gillick had been on board he would have selected someone else, but I wanted Roy," says Bavasi. "We went through the whole charade of attempting to create a search that summer, to play it up for publicity."

Bavasi put out a profile of what his first manager would be: a veteran, a teacher, a sound fundamental guy and someone who had managed at least at the Triple-A level. In other words, a guy like Roy Hartsfield.

The rumor mill worked overtime with names of possible managers. Names like Sparky Anderson and Dick Williams, who had both enjoyed success managing the Toronto Maple Leafs.

"There were all kinds of suggestions and all kinds of

names," says Bavasi. "No one realized the decision was pre-ordained years before."

Finally, the late Milton Richmond of United Press International broke the story. Toronto's first manager would be Roy Hartsfield, 52.

Hartsfield, an Atlanta, Ga. native, was part Wimp Sanderson, part Bobby Bragan and part Col. Sanders, fond of studding his conversation with down-home anecdotes and homespun aphorisms. All of which was mystifying to players from California, the inner city, Latin America and the north-east.

"Roy was perfect for our team at that point," says Bavasi. "We did a study on expansion managers and three years was about the limit. The only exception we found was Gene Mauch when he was in Montreal.

"Roy came out of the Dodger system, was very charming and with his terrific southern drawl was engaging to the community."

Engaging and puzzling.

Hector Torres, the Opening Day shortstop in 1977, played for Hartsfield the year before in Hawaii.

"He used to say 'The sun doesn't shine on the same dog every day,' which I think meant 'when it's finally your turn, don't screw it up,'" says Torres.

Outfielder Rick Bosetti didn't understand all of Hartsfield's quaint country slang, but then he doesn't remember hearing all of it either.

"In team meetings I'd leave, I mean mentally," admits Bosetti. "I'd just go off."

Bob Bailor, the Jays first pick in the expansion draft, has a similar memory.

"He was real big on meetings and would use all these southern sayings his grandpappy had told him," remembers Bob Bailor. "At the end of the team meeting he'd finish talking and we didn't have a clue as to why he had called the meeting.

"One meeting he said, 'Now say you're standing on one side of a fence and there is a mule on the other side. The mule keeps kicking you in the rear day after day. What do you do?' And then he walked out of the clubhouse."

Two years ago Bailor bumped into former Jay Willie Horton at an old-timers game and asked Horton: "Did you ever find out what to do about that mule who was kicking all of us from the other side of the fence?" Horton laughed and shook his head.

Horton hadn't figured it out. Neither had Bailor.

"It was tough enough for us to understand what Roy was saying or what he meant," says John Mayberry. "We had to try and figure out what he meant and then those of us who spoke Spanish passed it on to the Latins. We were always having meetings because we'd lose five, win two, lose six, win one, lose seven."

Balor Moore, a long tall Texan, knew Hartsfield-speak.

"Sure Roy had some Jethro, Jim Bob, or Ed Earl sayings, but I knew what he was talking about, I grew up with the same sayings," says Moore. "Just because Bobby Bailor wasn't quick enough to understand didn't mean we all didn't.

"What Roy was saying was if you're getting your brains beat out, you don't just stand there day after day and get kicked in the same place by the same mule. You move, you do what ever it takes to win."

Hartsfield concurred with Moore's assessment: "Whether we're in Artesia, New Mexico or Toronto, Canada, whether the classification is D ball or the major leagues, baseball is the same game. The bases are always 90 feet apart and it's a game of constant adjustments."

Purchased for the expansion fee of $7 million the Jays were consistent — consistently bad — on the field, their first three years with 107, 102 and 109 losses. They were equally as steady at the gate, drawing 1.7, 1.56 and 1.43 million fans to a park which had roughly 18,000 seats with chair backs in the baseball grandstand. Plenty used their Dominion coupons to sit in the outer reaches of the football grandstand where binoculars were a must.

In their first year of existence the Jays had 8,300 more season tickets than any other team in baseball, with exception of the Dodgers and Cincinnati.

Why did so many people come out to see a team lose so often? Well, the credit for marketing such a bad team so well goes to the workaholic Bavasi.

"It was a lot easier than people realize," says Bavasi. "Everything we did we looked at through the eye of the consumer, which is what I learned from (San Diego Padres owner) Ray Kroc. That was his approach with McDonald's restaurants."

The list of items for a team starting up were as long as Dave Lemancyzk's right arm and included such things as ticket prices, season tickets, sections, what would be sold at the concession stands and for how much, the start time of games, uniforms and the team logo.

Bavasi wanted the Jays insignia to be distinctive, to show the who, what and where of the team. To answer those three questions a red Maple Leaf, a two-colored Blue Jay, on a red baseball surrounded by Toronto Blue Jays script.

"Rather than just a simple letter 'T' we wanted something distinctive and more important, something we could license," says Bavasi.

The Jays almost landed in hot water when they showed AL president Lee MacPhail the original logo. MacPhail pointed out that it's against baseball's rules to have the image of a baseball on either a uniform or cap because it makes it more difficult for the hitter to pick up the flight of the ball.

"We looked at the logo without the baseball surrounding the bird and it didn't look very good," says Bavasi. "The AL office said that if any managers complained, we would have to remove the ball and go with something different."

Bavasi told MacPhail not to worry. He'd start the season with the new logo. If anyone complained, he'd switch to back-up caps which he had made. If anyone lodged a complaint about the baseball being on the uniform crest, Bavasi said he'd switch to different uniforms — which Bavasi says he didn't have.

"Fortunately for us, no one complained and the issue died," says Bavasi. "When you think of it, they weren't really going to get upset. We were headed to 107 losses. They weren't going to make us take our caps off and beat us too."

Still, the product on the field was borderline major league.

"The big thing about the new players is that they feel disenfranchised by their former team and most have a low self-image," says Bavasi. "The first year it was quite pronounced."

Bavasi went so far as to hire Dr. Bruce Ogilvie on a retainer as a sports psychologist. "It didn't work, mind you," Bavasi points out, "but we tried."

The budget for the 1977 Jays was a mere $5.2 million or about the same as what Jack Morris earned in 1992. Initial expenses were $1.3 million in payroll, $620,000 for transportation, $195,000 for spring training, stadium expenses $1 million, advertising $485,000, capital cost $1.3 million, scouting and minor league operations $500,000, uniforms $70,000 and $70,000 for tickets.

Small change now, but everything is relative and all were sizable investments when the Jays were born.

Bavasi had some hard and fast rules from another era, such as a policy against long hair and unruly facial hair. The club also banned women reporters from the clubhouse and the team charter. Beards were allowed in year four and women gained equal rights a few seasons later.

The Toronto *Sun* ran a telephone poll to see what its readers thought of the hair edict. A few days later an internal memo found its way to the *Sun*. In it Bavasi asked staffers to call the *Sun* and announce their support of the policy but not to identify themselves as club employees. Talk about trying to manipulate the media!

When the memo was printed in the *Sun*, much to the embarrassment of the image-conscious Blue Jays. Bavasi retorted: "The *Sun* is to their medium what *Mad* magazine is to their medium."

Policies weren't the only reasons people railed about the Blue Jays. Outfielder John Lowenstein went up to Bavasi after the first spring workout and said it was the most disorganized camp he had ever seen. He predicted the organization wouldn't go anywhere. He was dealt to Cleveland within a month, wanting no part of the lopsided losses and losing streaks.

"We were at a distinct disadvantage," says Hartsfield. "We had youngsters who weren't ready, guys who weren't given another chance by their previous organization and players coming off injuries.

"But we gave them the canoe. It was up to them to do the paddling."

Most of it was upstream.

Shortstop Hector Torres played for Houston in 1969 when Montreal and San Diego were admitted to the National League.

"We lost the first game San Diego ever played and we were embarrassed," says Torres. "I'm sure it was the same when the Blue Jays started playing. If one of the established teams lost, it was like a mistake had happened."

Torres has been with the Blue Jays since Day One. Playing at Syracuse in 1978 and being a coach at one level or another ever since.

Left-hander Tommy Underwood recalls arriving in Toronto to start the 1978 season.

"I remember driving in on the bus from the airport," says Tom Underwood. "It was about 10 at night. Bo (Rick Bosetti) and I gave the city about 10 minutes and decided we didn't like it.

"When we woke up in the morning and saw the city in the daylight, we realized it was no different from the U.S. In fact, it was better. I'd been in Montreal with the Phillies and Toronto is a much nicer city. I guess we were just in a pissy mood. I think we'd opened in Detroit and were beaten pretty bad."

When Bosetti arrived in 1978 at spring training, he was wearing a T-shirt which read: "Toronto at last."

And last they were.

Left-hander Balor Moore remembers the need to win lying with the other team.

"How'd you like to be the Yankees, sitting in first place ahead of us by roughly 100 games and into town we come? In 1978, Billy Martin's first game back, one of his many first games back, we went in there for a doubleheader," says Moore. "Tommy Underwood lost the first game by a run and I beat them in the nightcap. Two complete games.

"When you're playing on a bad team you become a little bit more self-centred and losing 100 games made each one of us think of our own stats so we could talk contract the next year. We didn't put the team first like the World Series team did."

Playing established teams, which was everyone but Seattle, wasn't any walk in the park.

"Every day was a different game and you'd set different goals for yourself," recalls Bosetti. "Like I'd say, 'I'm going to throw out someone from centre field.' Or, 'I'm going to get two hits today.' And if I do, maybe we win.

"Sometimes a buddy from another team would come up and say 'Oh man, that's gotta be tough playing for this team.' Hey, at least I was playing. What it was, was a chance to establish yourself as a big leaguer."

Bosetti was one of the few major leaguers who made the city his year-round home during his playing days. That and his other on-field antics made him a fan favorite.

"My best memories of baseball are playing in Toronto," says Bosetti. "The Blue Jays gave me the opportunity to play. Toronto was the best city I ever played in — the quality of the people, the cleanliness and it was a safe city. That's why I lived there year round."

A native of Redding, Calif., Bosetti lived in a condominium at Burnhamthorpe and Mill Road, the same Mississauga building where former Argo coach Leo Cahill lived. Still, he was frustrated the Jays didn't chase any free agents to improve the club at a quicker pace.

"Back then the Jays were making a lot of money," says Bosetti. "You look at the team now, with a payroll of $45 million or whatever, and they're packing in four million fans a year and they're making a lot of money.

"In those years with a payroll of a couple of million and they're drawing 1.5 to 2 million at the gate. You tell me they weren't making money back then? Now that the team's been in the league longer and with the SkyDome, 90 per cent of the players would want to play in Toronto."

But not then. Then they wanted to play *against* Toronto.

"Every time you won, it was a game the other team shouldn't have lost," remembers Bailor. "Like we'd play, say, the Yankees or the Red Sox in a four-game series and we managed to win a game, it was like they should have won all four. The feeling was *they shouldn't have lost to us."*

Years later Moore, 12-17 lifetime as a Jay, talks with his chest stuck out, sounding as if he's the proudest member of the young team's alumni association.

"The darned World Series games last fall were on so late it was tough to stay awake, even in the Central Time zone," says Moore from Houston. "I was so tired a couple of nights, I watched the final two innings standing. They teach you that in the army. You can't fall asleep if you're on your feet."

He rejoiced as the uniform he wore through two 100-loss seasons was now soaked in champagne.

"The team built a tradition by bringing us back on a steady basis," says Moore. "We've bonded. The friendships we have now are stronger than when we were playing.

"I can't say enough about how strongly I feel for the organization without sounding corny."

The friendships formed those first years have been fostered by get-togethers at JaysFest and Upper Deck Old Timers games at SkyDome, as well as the Fantasy Camp in Dunedin. They don't sit and talk about the 13-1 losses. Sometimes, says Moore, the pump has to be primed — with a couple of beers — and the stories start to flow. He says, "The only thing I missed was playing on a championship team. Of course, with my kind of career I wouldn't have been on a team with that type of talent."

One strong friendship that has developed is between Bob Bailor, known as Little Bailor (five-foot-nine) and Balor Moore (six-foot-three), called Big Balor.

"The only reason he got married is because she thought she was marrying me," jokes Moore in reference to the similarity in names.

Counters Bailor: "Least my name is spelled correctly. Everyone knows they are a little slower down in Texas."

One of their stories: The Jays followed the Orioles into Comiskey Park the night after the infamous "Disco Demolition" night, an ill-starred promotion in which fans were invited to bring their old disco albums to the ballpark for destruction. The fans got a little out of hand, forcing cancellation of the second game of a doubleheader when a fire broke out on the field. A rain storm made the field more suitable for marine maneuvers rather than a major-league game.

"The Orioles pulled their team off, wouldn't play the night before," Moore remembers. "The conditions weren't too bad for the Toronto Blue Jays. I pitched and Little Bailor was out there trying to play right field. The sand was so deep it came up over the tops of his shoes. He put a little flag on the back of his hat just in case he fell in a hole out there, we'd be able to find him."

The White Sox prevailed, knocking out Moore thanks to a couple of elements-aided hits. A bloop single into shallow right wound up being a two-run triple.

"Little Bailor spun his wheels when they hit this little lame duck, then he came slogging in, dove, just missed and the ball plunked in the sand. Didn't roll an inch. I think if a regular-sized person had been out there instead of Little Bailor, he would have caught the ball."

Says Little Bailor: "If he hadn't have been pitching and someone else was out there, all the outfielders wouldn't have had to have their backs pinned against the wall to make leaping catches."

Big Balor has only one bad memory of his Jays days. Manager Bobby Mattick, who succeeded Hartsfield following the 1979 season, called the erratic lefty into his office in 1980 and told him the club was making a change.

Moore moved into baseball's afterlife and now, instead of bailing cotton, chopping wood or milking cows as the generation of retiring pros before him was wont to do, runs a successful steel pipe company,

He eagerly awaits invitations from the Jays to attend various functions and the opportunity to stand up in front of the TV to watch a late-night post-season game again.

FIFTH INNING

◆1. The Jays dealt Jorge Orta to Kansas City for Willie Mays Aikens in December 1983. But Willie Aikens was unable to make spring training with the Jays in 1984 due to a prior engagement. Why?

◆2. Which Blue Jay once quarterbacked his college football team to three Rose Bowls and turned down contract offers from the Denver Broncos?

◆3. Although this Blue Jay sports an ERA of 27 for his only mound appearance, he was selected Labatt's Player of the Game for his inning in the spotlight on August 15, 1984. Name him.

◆4. Who holds the team record for steals in a season?

◆5. The Jays grabbed these two prospects in the '84 major league draft and had to keep them on their major league roster in '85, sometimes cited as a factor behind the Jays' eventual demise in the playoffs. Name the players.

◆6. In 1985 the Jays finally got the stopper they'd been looking for — Tom Henke. Ironically, he was given the number of a previous reliever whose propensity for blowing saves would often send manager Bobby Cox screaming into the showers after a game. Name him.

◆7. How did the Jays acquire Tom Henke?

◆8. Closer Bill Caudill was expected to be the Jays' savior in 1985, but for the most part he was a disappointment. Still, he did set a new team record — what was it?

◆9. Perhaps the greatest bargain in this era of multi-million dollar contracts was former Jay pitcher Doyle Alexander. Over four seasons he racked up a 46-26 record and for most of that time, the lion's share of his salary was paid by another team — which one?

◆10. Al Oliver was added to the Jays' lineup mid-way through the '85 season, and is best remembered for his clutch hits in the ALCS. What was his uniform number?

◆11. The 1985 AL East pennant race came down to the second last game, when the Jays clinched their first division championship over the Yankees by beating them 5-1 at Exhibition Stadium. By clinching it that afternoon, and by averting a first place tie, it meant the Jays would not have to make up an earlier game against the Orioles which was postponed. Why was this August date with the Orioles originally cancelled?

◆12. The image is still there — the Jays clinch the '85 AL East championship as George Bell puts the squeeze on a fly ball to left. Who hit it?

◆13. This veteran Yankees pitcher won his 300th career game the day after the Jays clinched their first AL East championship — name him.

◆14. If the Jays had won the World Series in 1985, it might have been termed a miracle for a ninth-year team. One member of the Jays' organization knew all about miraculous World Series wins, having played for the '69 Mets. Who was he?

◆15. As the Jays were about to square off against the Kansas City Royals for the American League Championship, Chicago sportswriter Ron Berler insisted the Jays didn't have a prayer — they were afflicted with the dreaded "X Factor." What was it?

◆16. This rookie catcher, with only four games of major league experience, filled in behind the plate for three innings during the 1985 ALCS when Ernie Whitt was lifted for pinch hitters. Who was he?

◆17. In Game 7 of the 1985 ALCS, this Royal hit the infamous "wind-blown" triple over Jesse Barfield's head that salted the game, and league championship, away. Who was he?

◆18. During the course of the 1985 ALCS, the Jays used every player on their bench but one. Who got the splinters?

◆19. This Royal hit three home runs during the 1985 ALCS, and almost single-handedly won game three for them, going 4-for-4 and scoring 3 RBIs. Name him.

◆20. If the 1985 Jays-Royals championship series had been played the year before, the Jays would have made their first trip to the World Series. Why?

Answers begin on page 148.

THE MISTAKE BY THE LAKE
CHAPTER FIVE

George Bell remembers the first time he ever laid eyes on it like it was yesterday.

So do Rick Bosetti, John Mayberry and Balor Moore. Ah yes, Exhibition Stadium!

Just saying the words brings a chill to the spine. For some loyal Blue Jays fans from the early years, sitting on a frozen aluminum bleacher bench down the right field line season after season may have left more permanent reminders.

As a baseball park, Exhibition Stadium wasn't a bad football stadium. Let's just say Exhibition Stadium wasn't so named because it was a perfect exhibit of the modern-day stadia.

"This is temporary, isn't it? I mean, it won't be like this when we start playing, will it?" Bell asked Alfredo Griffin, after walking out of the clubhouse for his first viewing in 1981. "It wasn't even as good as some of the minor-league parks. I thought temporary, like for maybe a few weeks but he said we'd be playing here for more like a few years."

It was part wildlife sanctuary, part wind tunnel and since it was sometimes used as a football field, the artificial turf was also part rolling hills and part bumps and grinds.

"The turf was like shooting marbles in a bath tub," says Bosetti. "I took a look around and thought: 'This is a big-league stadium?'"

Says Mayberry: "It was different, plenty of lumps, bumps and humps."

A ballboy covers the corpse of the seagull done in by Dave Winfield in 1983. Sunglare, snow, sleet and seagulls were hazards at the Ex.
photo: Hans Deryk/Toronto Sun Archives

Most nights, as the sun set leisurely behind the left field grandstand, fans down the first-base line could finally open their eyes wide again, and forget about squinting and toweling off the perspiration created by the blinding afternoon sun.

An inning later as the wind began to whip, it was suddenly sweater and jacket weather, just as it had been for the fans on the third base line at game time.

Nowadays baseball is described as a game of business, and outside of Bay Street, the largest centre for business meetings in Toronto is SkyDome, particularly at the SkyBox level. It wasn't always that way, especially when the suits went to see a ball game at Exhibition Stadium.

Remembers one businessman, "We were on the aisle a few rows up from the end of the dugout for a night game. I make the mistake of sitting in the second seat in and giving my client the seat on the aisle.

"He was pleased about going to the game, but we didn't hit it off that well. I was trying to talk business with him, but looking into the sun, with Nolan Ryan grunting, throwing fastballs and all of Toronto's right-handed hitters fouling pitches our way ... well, it was awfully difficult to establish any constant eye contact. I was so afraid of getting hit in the side of the head with a line drive I couldn't look him in the eye."

Needless to say, the attempted sale was much like many Blue Jay rallies those early years — unfinished.

By contrast, construction on the stadium *was* finished — it just didn't look that way. Just as the constant change of the outfield grandstand at Arlington Stadium in Texas affected how far the ball would travel, so did the football grandstand affect the course of a Jays' contest.

Because of the park's configuration — the 100-year-old grandstand had been home to football and concert crowds during the CNE, while a smaller grandstand abutted the lakeshore — the wind would whistle and swirl and curl on its way to Lake Ontario.

"Exhibition reminded me of Candlestick Park the way the wind blew so much," says Opening Day shortstop Hector Torres. "The day games were all right, but at night it could get cold and windy very quickly."

Battling the winds more often than anyone this side of Lloyd Moseby was Bosetti.

"After a while I developed a love-hate relationship with it," says Bosetti. "But it was a tough place to play."

C'mon, how tough could it be?

"Well, you had to run uphill to left centre and downhill to right centre," claims Bosetti, referring to the crown in the football field for drainage during football season. You can't have the middle of a football field under water. Therefore the field sloped towards each sideline or, shall we say, the football grandstand and the area in back of second base.

"It was rough for our middle infielders, but almost impossible for a visiting player," says John Mayberry. "I don't know how many players I'd see turn their backs, look up at the ball, stumble and fall running down the slight slope into centre."

Stationed at first, Big John didn't have to worry about the slope.

You've heard about basketball teams knowing the dead spots in a court or hockey players knowing the bounces off the end boards or what the puck will do off the glass? Well, Jays outfielders had to know the rolls and contours along with the ever-changing winds.

"It was a fun place to watch players from the other team try and play centre field," chuckles Bosetti. "Watching Fred Lynn was my favorite. He had no idea how to play it. He'd stand three feet from the warning track. He'd look up at right-field foul pole and the flag would be blowing in. Then he'd look across at left-field foul pole and the flags there would be blowing in too."

Obviously the wind can't blow in from both left and right at the same time and this was a problem for visiting players, even though Lynn was considered one of the best ever at his position.

"From our dugout you'd look out at Lynn and you could only see him from the waist up, he was playing so deep," says lefty Tommy Underwood.

While pitchers had their reservations about performing in a wind tunnel, Mayberry had just left spacious Royals

Stadium in Kansas City, a place where home runs died on the warning track. He took a look around and licked his chops. Both Royals and Exhibition were 330 feet (100m) down the right-field line. But while it was 385 feet (118m) to right centre and 410 (125m) to centre in Kansas City, at Exhibition the signs read 375 feet (115m) to right centre and 400 (120m) to straightaway centre. What the signs didn't reveal was the forecast: prevailing wind to straight-away right, gusting at times.

Mayberry knew what to expect when the Royals sold his contract to the Jays April 4, 1978. He was the first player to register a three-homer game at Exhibition the year before. And Big John picked on three different pitchers: Mike Willis, Jerry Johnson and Tom Bruno.

"The turf might have been bad but I'm not going to knock the stadium, I *luuuuved* that right field fence," says Mayberry today from Kansas City. "It was a hitter's park and from the top of the inning until the third out the wind could change. Those guys in the outfield had to be on their toes.

"If Garth Iorg can hit out two homers to right field, there *has* to be some kind of wind blowing that way."

Although the Jays as a team played dismally in 1978 and 1979, Mayberry and team-mate Rico Carty made things interesting by staging their own race for team home run king.

Mayberry says he won the home run contest 22-20. Carty disputes those totals since they were long-distance shots hit while in a Jays uniform. Carty hit 11 more while with Oakland for a 31-22 advantage. In 1979 the Dominican dandy was back with the Jays, but Mayberry outhomered him 21-12.

"The Big Mon talked loud and said nothing, he had this big old booming voice," says Mayberry, not exactly a shrinking violet, himself. "If you heard the walls trembling you'd hear him coming. I think they could hear him in Timbuktu. He pushed me and I pushed him. He'd hit a homer and I'd try to match him."

In those days, the Jays who went over the fence later could go out to eat for free.

"Trader Vic's used to give you a lobster dinner for two if you hit a homer," says Mayberry, who didn't do too badly in 1980, after Carty departed a second and final time. "I had 15 homers for Bobby Mattick by the all-star break. Bobby knew I was a 10-year veteran. He let me progress at my own speed, as long as I produced."

Big John produced a lot and so often he would give away free dinners to coaches like Jackie Moore, Don Leppert and John Felske. That was a partial thanks to the coaches who got him rolling with fat pitches during batting practice.

There were other home-run hitting, lobster-eating maniacs on the Blue Jays. After the 1981 season, the club's fifth, Mayberry was the career leader on the all-time list with 90 homers. He was followed by Otto (The Swatto) Velez with 71 and Roy Howell with 43.

"Just a great hitter, but Otto could get hurt quicker than you could say 'Jack Rabbit,'" says Mayberry. "I remember one night Roy Hartsfield sent him up to pinch hit. He got as far as the on-deck circle."

Velez took a couple of practice swings with the lead pipe bat most hitters use while warming up then stopped suddenly. When his at-bat came, Velez switched directions and headed not for the batter's box, but to the Jays dugout, a pained look on his face. Hartsfield had to use a pinch hitter for his scheduled pinch hitter.

"Another night we're playing in Seattle," Mayberry recalls, "they've got a man on second and a guy singles to left where Otto's playing. Otto comes charging in, he's got a play at the plate and he's ready to throw the guy out.

"Just as he fields the ball he steps on his glove and down he goes. He pulled something in his leg."

On May 4, 1980 Velez showed Mayberry how to go deep in style, finding his stroke and the Exhibition Stadium jetstream at the same time. He became the first Jay to homer three times, in the first game of a doubleheader against the Indians, tying an AL record. He homered again in the nightcap. Four homers. All in a day's work.

He hit a grand slam over the centre field fence in the opener off Dan Spillner, homered again and in the bottom of the 10th his solo shot made the Jays 9-8 winners. In the second game he lined a three-run homer to start the Jays on their way to a 7-2 victory.

Four homers and 10 RBIs. This was not a lobster night. Mayberry and Alvis Woods took Velez to the popular Underground Railroad restaurant after the game for African-American cuisine.

"My friend and good buddy Big John Henry was running the place," says Big John Mayberry, revealing an early sign of Jaysmania. "We want in and Big John Henry was so excited about Otto's four homers that when he saw Otto he told his staff, 'Hey, this here is Otto Velez! Get him anything he wants! Oh yeah, and get the same for those other two guys.'

"Al and I were regulars, we went there all the time and Big John Henry was so excited he couldn't even remember our names. Can you imagine?"

In 1985, Seattle school teacher Bob Wood wrote a book named *Dodger Dogs to Fenway Franks*. He rated the parks based on seating, food, atmosphere, facilities and sightlines. To no one's surprise, Exhibition Stadium ranked dead last.

Yet when told of the survey, the old Jays become suddenly protective of their first home.

Balor Moore says that while the stadium was far from pretty, he was happy to be there.

"It was a fantastic clubhouse, the dugouts were fine and, hey, it was the major leagues," remembers Moore. "I wasn't complaining."

"The clubhouse was nice and roomy," says Mayberry. "And with that right-field fence there, wasn't anything I could complain about. It wasn't that cold. With the Royals early in the year, we'd go on a Cleveland-Toronto-Chicago road trip and you couldn't say one place was colder than the other."

"Even though it was the worst place I ever played, I have fond memories," says Tom Henke. "I remember my first game in 1985. I'd been called up from Syracuse when the team was in Baltimore. I had a couple of wins and a save in four games. The fans of Toronto had never even seen me. Bobby Cox brought me in and the fans at Exhibition Stadium gave me a standing ovation. That relaxed me.

When I'm done, I'll look back on that day as one of my greatest memories in baseball."

A lot of nights the Jays were like mailmen, trying to make their appointed rounds through wind, rain, fog, snow and sleet.

How windy was it? Well, you've all heard about Stu Miller being blown off the mound at Candlestick Park and Hector Torres comparing the Ex to the 'Stick.

On April 30, 1984 the Jays breezed in and out of work against the Texas Rangers. Right-hander Jim Clancy's stint on the mound lasted precisely two minutes and two batters before the game was called on account of wind. Two days before in Kansas City, Clancy had had his start rained out. "If it's not one thing it's another," he said.

Clancy retired the first two Rangers on five pitches. Afterwards in the clubhouse Ernie Whitt presented him with a congratulatory beer. "It's the third perfect game I've caught," joked Whitt.

"Continuing play would have made a travesty of the game," said crew chief Don Denkinger. "It would have done more harm than good. I didn't think we should've started anyway."

After a half an hour wait Denkinger called the game, the Jays had the night off and the first "wind-out" went into the record books.

Balor Moore remembers a game in 1978 which should have been called by rain and wasn't.

"We played four or five innings in a steady rain," recalls Moore. "It was an afternoon but it was so dark and gloomy the lights were turned on. Finally the rain stopped and the sun came out. We continued to play but as the sun hit the wet carpet steam began to come off the turf."

That was too much.

"The outfielders couldn't see the infielders and the infielders couldn't see the catcher," says Moore. "They called the game — on account of steam. So we played in rain and couldn't play when the hot sun was shining. I remember saying 'If I haven't seen everything now.'

"I'd played all over Canada, in Montreal, Winnipeg, Quebec City and Vancouver, but that was the first time I'd ever seen anything that strange."

On May 5, 1981 a deep fog moved in off the lake and forced cancellation of a game between the Jays and Indians. On April 15, 1988 the Jays-Twins game was canceled because of cold. Another game was suspended when Kelly Gruber's routine fly ball was lost in the fog for an inside-the-park homer.

The strangest sight of all at the old yard occurred on August 4, 1983.

The Yankees' Dave Winfield was warming up in right field, playing catch with the ball boy down the right field line, the way most outfielders spend time during commercial breaks. It's a ritual as old as the game itself.

As the infield ball was tossed into the dugout and Winfield turned to do the same, Winfield threw the ball to the waiting ball boy on a bounce. The ball beaned a sea gull that had been standing in foul territory. The bird was killed instantly — the first and only death on the field of Exhibition Stadium.

Instead of resuming his position on a chair down the right field line, the ball boy hustled out with a towel and took the bird off the field for proper burial.

This wasn't the end of the story. A Toronto police officer who watched what had happened suspected foul play regarding the fowl. In other words, he suspected that Winfield had aimed at the bird intentionally.

"Intentional?" scoffed Billy Martin after the Yankees had won 3-1. "They wouldn't say that if they'd seen the way he's been throwing. He hasn't hit a cutoff man all year."

Winfield was hauled off to the station house to be booked. Executive vice-president Pat Gillick accompanied Winfield to the station and then sped him to the airport where the Yankee charter was waiting.

The next day red-faced city official dropped the charges. Martin suggested the gull be shipped to Yankee Stadium and be buried within the centre-field monuments, "right alongside the Babe."

Once he was over the initial shock, Winfield made an off-season peace offering. He commissioned a painting in his home town of Minneapolis for sale to the highest bidder.

At the annual Easter Seals dinner in Toronto the painting sold for $32,000, all of which helped make Winfield one of the most popular visiting players.

Jackie Moore has worked the last three stadiums where pro baseball has been played in Toronto. In 1967, the last year of Maple Leaf Stadium, he managed the Maple Leafs' final month.

Ten years later Moore was at Exhibition Stadium Opening Day as a coach with the Blue Jays. In 1991, he was back as a member of Lou Piniella's Cincinnati Reds coaching staff attending the All-Star Game.

"The thing I remember about Opening Day, besides the fact that it snowed and I was sure we wouldn't play in those conditions, was how the place looked empty even though it was packed," said Moore. "You'd look up in the seats and you couldn't see any faces. People had ski masks or were wearing parkas covering all but their eyes.

"We couldn't see them but as soon as Doug Ault started hitting homers there was plenty of people jumping around."

Moore isn't the only early Jay who says he wishes he had the chance to play at SkyDome.

"Home run hitters *luuuuve* decked stadiums, it's something to shoot for," says Mayberry. "You can see where the ball lands rather than just going off into the night somewhere.

"I'd have luuved to shoot for those decks in the SkyDome. Like that one Jose Canseco hit off Mike Flanagan into (the fifth deck) or when I was at Olympic Stadium for an Old-Timers game. I stood at home plate and looked up into the 300 level where all the seats were red except one that was painted yellow. That's where old Willie Stargell homered. I couldn't believe anyone could hit a ball that far."

In many ways Exhibition Stadium was a paradox, loved by regulars who got their big break there, despised by visitors who were looking for something else.

And in the final game ever played there, May 28, 1989, against the White Sox, the two extremes were never more in evidence.

For the final, pre-game festivities, players were introduced. When George Bell was introduced, he was booed lustily. Bell had been the most booed man at the park for years, so why should things change now? Well, feelings changed in the bottom of the 10th when Kelly Gruber led off with a double against Bobby Thigpen and Bell followed by hitting a 0-1 pitch half-way up into the football grandstand.

Like the opening contest, the curtain came down with a win over the White Sox, this one a 7-5 triumph.

"With an exciting win like that, it was a great way to leave," said Bob Brenly, "but come to think of it, I can't think of a bad way to leave here."

SIXTH INNING

♦1. Who was the first player to represent the Blue Jays at the Major League All-Star Game in 1977?

♦2. Who was the first Toronto Blue Jays pitcher selected to play for the American League in the All-Star Game?

♦3. Two Blue Jay third basemen have made appearances in the All-Star Game. Kelly Gruber is one of them, chosen in 1989 and 1990. Who was the other?

♦4. When Dave Stieb made his seventh All-Star Game appearance in 1990, he tied the record for most appearances by an AL hurler. Who shares the record?

♦5. Dave Stieb's first All-Star Game was not a memorable one — in fact, his performance tied him with Juan Marichal in what dubious category?

♦6. Who was the first Blue Jay to get a hit in the All-Star Game?

♦7. Who was the first Blue Jay voted by fan ballot to the AL team?

♦8. Which Blue Jay pitcher has made two plate appearances in the All-Star Game?

◆9. In the 1984 All-Star Game, this Montreal Expo hit a home run off Dave Stieb in the second inning — name him.

◆10. This Blue Jay tied Willie Mays' record for most steals in a single All-Star Game, even though he didn't get a hit. Name him?

◆11. True or false: the 1991 All-Star Game in Toronto marked the first time the mid-season classic was held outside the United States.

◆12. Who was the winning pitcher of the 1991 All-Star Game in Toronto?

◆13. In 1976, Cleveland reliever Dave LaRoche was the first pitcher without a win to his credit to be selected to the American League All-Star team. Eleven years later, this Jays pitcher became the second — who was he?

◆14. Who, of the following list of Jay greats, never represented Toronto at the All-Star Game: Tony Fernandez, Fred McGriff, George Bell?

Answers begin on page 150.

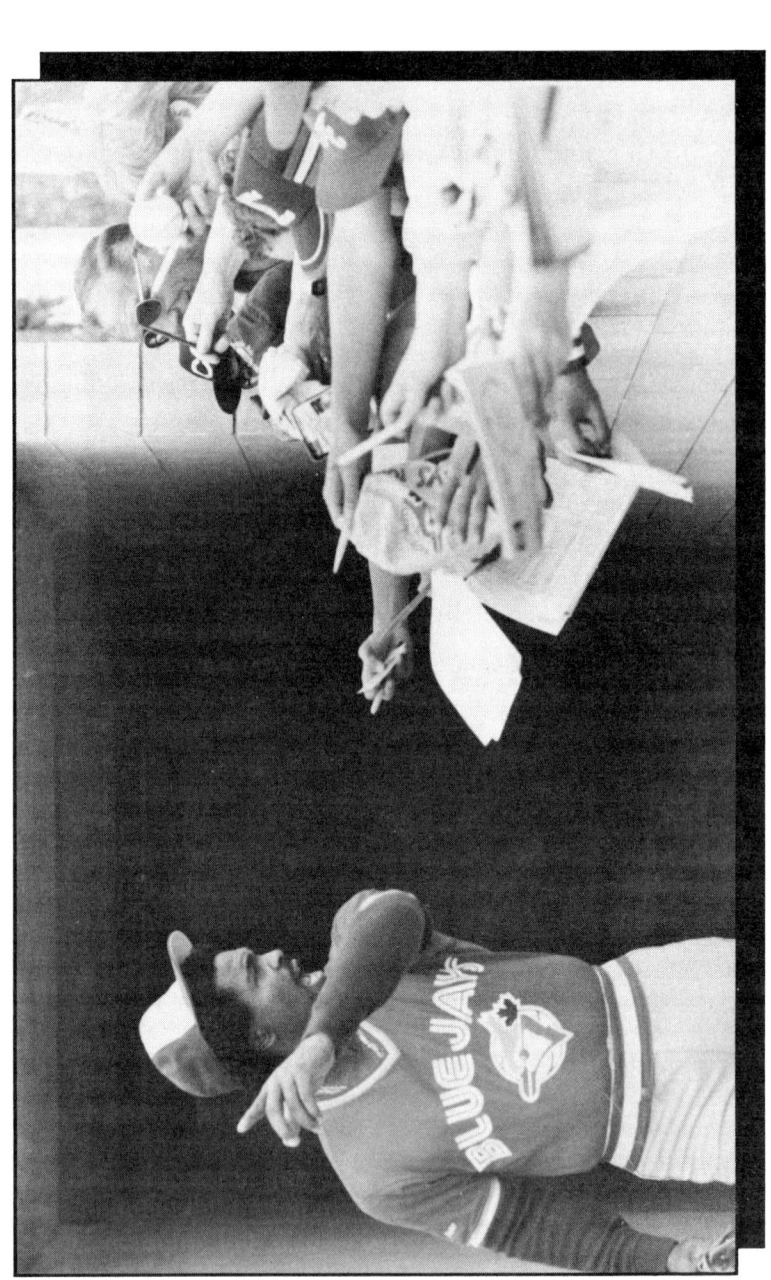

Outfielder George Bell had an often stormy relationship with Blue Jay fans, even during his MVP season in 1987.
photo: Veronica Milne/Toronto Sun

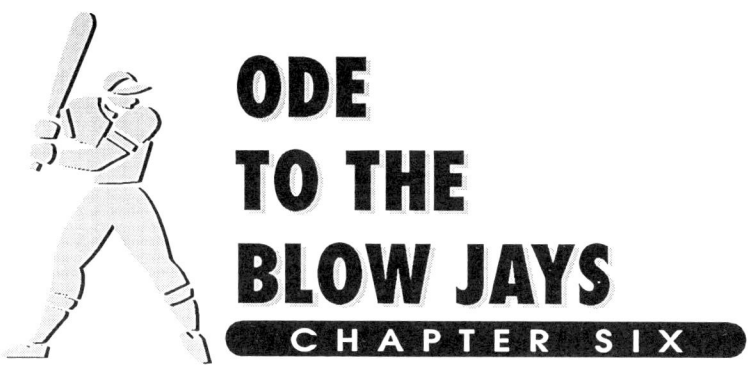

ODE TO THE BLOW JAYS
CHAPTER SIX

Dr. William Mills was the winner of the Name the Team contest back in 1976.

His suggestion to call Toronto's expansion franchise the Blue Jays was selected from among 4,000 different names and more than 30,000 entries.

A decade later sarcastic fans, TV talking heads and writers had given the team a new, derisive moniker.

In 1985, the Blue Jays were leading the Kansas City Royals 3-1 in the American League Championship Series. With the final two games at home, they lost the series in the seventh game. In 1987, the Blue Jays dropped their final seven games to lose the American League East division to the Detroit Tigers.

As a result, they were referred to as the "Blow Jays." As in give them a lead and they'll blow it.

No prizes were awarded for coming up with this nickname.

While 1985 could be written off as a "growing experience" for a young team, 1987 was a collapse which ranked with Gene Mauch's Philadelphia Phillies disastrous breakdown in 1964.

Heading into their game on the second last Sunday of the regular schedule, the Jays owned a 3-1/2 game lead over the rival Tigers, thanks to a trio of wins in the first three matches of a four-game series at Exhibition Stadium. In fact, they were three outs away from owning a 4-1/2 game lead with only six games to play, while the Tigers had seven remaining.

Sounds like a pretty insurmountable lead, doesn't it?

Well, Kirk Gibson homered off Tom Henke leading off the ninth and when the dust settled on the long afternoon the Tigers had a 3-2 victory. The lead was at 2-1/2 games.

Milwaukee came into Exhibition Stadium and swept the Jays, while the Tigers were splitting a four-game series in Baltimore. So that meant it all came down to the final weekend, a three-game series in Detroit. The Jays dropped all three straight games and it was over.

Looking back at the big picture, the final seven games between the Jays and the Tigers were all one-run decisions. Great baseball if you were a purist. A terrible end to a great season if you were a Blue Jays fan. Either way, the Blue Jays had finished with a whimper, not with a bang and gone a long way to living up to their new nickname.

What about the injuries, you say? Well, yes, shortstop Tony Fernandez missed the final 10 games after being upended in a collision at second base which fractured his right elbow. And Ernie Whitt tried to be too aggressive against Brewers second baseman Paul Molitor. Whitt rammed Molitor and wound up cracking a pair of ribs. He missed the final four games.

Baseball is a team game, though, and the Blue Jays, or at least the other seven hitters, should have been able to overcome the loss of Fernandez and Whitt to win at least *one* of the final seven games.

What would have happened to the managerial career of Jimy Williams if the Jays had won that final weekend in Detroit? Both players and fans lost confidence in Williams. Only management backed him.

Would the Jays have grown into a dynasty had they won the division and advanced against the Minnesota Twins, whom they had handled all year?

What if MVP George Bell hadn't finished in the depths of a 2-for-26 slump which included an infield single? What if part-timers Cecil Fielder and Manny Lee hadn't missed signals that final weekend in Detroit? What if Williams had used Tom Henke Saturday afternoon in a tie game rather than Jeff Musselman?

As you can see and as you well remember, there were plenty of questions and few answers. The answers didn't matter — Detroit had won and Toronto had lost.

Losing 100 games was one thing, but losing the division on the final day of the 162-day season was something else entirely for Blue Jays fans to endure. Dyed-in-the wool Jays supporters could relate to the late commissioner A. Bartlett Giammatti, who once said, "The game is meant to break your heart."

So where to start when looking back at 1987?

Yes, the final week was a blow, but for that loss to have meant so much, the Jays had to have created some incredible expectations.

On June 2, the Jays were roaring with a club-record 11-game win streak. Thanks to a 'Vote George' campaign, George Bell had become the first Toronto player ever voted to a starting position in the All-Star Game. With the Jays playing the Royals in the final game before the break, a plane pulling a banner circled Exhibition Stadium. "Thanks fans — George" was its simple message. Roy Firestone suggested the idea to Bell, whose relationship with the fans bordered on love-hate even during his MVP season.

In a game August 15, the Jays beat Cleveland 15-1 to bump the Yankees out of first for the first time since June. Yet the Tigers were coming hard.

On September 14, the once-proud Orioles, bound for a 100-loss season, came to Exhibition Stadium. The Blue Jays lumber company laid a beating on the rival birds. Toronto hitters slugged a major-league record 10 homers. Whitt hit three homers in the 18-3 victory, against loser Ken Dixon. Rance Mulliniks and George Bell had a pair each. Lloyd Moseby, Fred McGriff and Rob Ducey had the others. To this day a huge autographed picture celebrating the exploits of the six sluggers hangs in manager Cito Gaston's office. He was the hitting instructor at the time.

Later that month the Jays returned to Memorial Stadium for a three-game series in Baltimore. This time there was no Ken Dixon, but still plenty of heroics from Bell. The first night Bell singled off Mike Boddicker to bring home Lloyd Moseby in the ninth and provide the Jays with a 2-1 win.

The next night the score was tied 3-3 in the eighth when Bell doubled home Moseby with the tie-breaking run. And in the finale he hit a two-run homer in the fifth.

And now the Jays came home to play the Tigers for the first time in 74 games. Back then they were six games back. This time as the Detroit bus pulled into foul territory down the right field line with Tigers in their tank, they were trailing by half a game.

A memorable four game series was about to unfold. Would it decide the season or just make next weekend all the more important?

With Thursday night's game scoreless in the third, Mike Flanagan was facing Jack Morris and Tiger Bill Madlock was leading on first base. Kirk Gibson bounced to second baseman Nelson Liriano who flipped to Fernandez coming across the bag for the force. There wasn't a double play. Nor was there a return throw to first.

Madlock caught Fernandez's legs with a roll block; the fragile shortstop flipped in mid-air and landed with a thud. It might not have been that bad had Fernandez landed on the dirt or the artificial turf. However, Fernandez's elbow came down on the metal frame of the square, cut-out portion of the artificial turf for second base. Not an ideal landing pad under any circumstances.

Manny Lee took over at shortstop for Fernandez. About the same time Whitt scored from third on a Morris wild pitch in the eighth inning, Fernandez was having surgery performed on his right elbow.

Now up a half game, Lee was in the starting lineup the next night. As always happens when an established player goes down, the spotlight shone on his replacement. Sometimes bows and applause accompany the novice's start, but more often it's a case of showing the difference between the veteran and the kid.

Frank Tanana had the Jays on the ropes throwing nothing but zeros. In the ninth, with the Jays trailing 2-0, Jesse Barfield singled off reliever Dickie Noles and pinch hitter Rick Leach followed with a double off Willie Hernandez.

With only one out, Lee tripled down the right field line to tie the game.

Manager Sparky Anderson asked Mike Henneman to walk the next batter intentionally, but rather than loading the bases, he decided to pitch to Lloyd Moseby. Moseby bounced a hard smash to second baseman Lou Whitaker, who hesitated, considered throwing to second and then decided to throw home. He bounced his throw in the dirt, Lee scored and now the Jays were up by 1-1/2 games.

Finally, the big bats came out of storage on Saturday afternoon. The Tigers appeared to be home and cooled out with a 9-4 lead, but once again the Detroit bullpen wound up with a blown save.

Juan Beniquez, picked up from Kansas City at the All-Star break, hit a three-run double in the bottom of the ninth to decide matters. Now the lead was 2-1/2 games. While the Blue Jays hustled out into the night to celebrate their good fortune, the veteran Tigers slowly gravitated to a picnic table in the visitor's clubhouse.

"Maybe the Jays should enjoy this while they can," said Kirk Gibson. "We may be setting the biggest bear trap of all time. We're not known for rolling over."

Darrell Evans. Alan Trammell. Dave Bergman. Kirk Gibson. Doyle Alexander. Jack Morris. They all gathered around the picnic table for a few beers to talk things out for a confidence builder. "If we could only win tomorrow," seemed to be said more than once.

"We didn't feel very good about ourselves when the game ended," said Evans. "We had some things to talk about. We weren't going to leave until we felt better."

The Tigers showed up on Sunday with Doyle Alexander on the mound and thousands of 'Foil Doyle' Toronto *Sun* inserts waving at him. Alexander had departed Toronto for Atlanta on a stream of anger directed at both the city and the team. There was too much post-game traffic. He didn't like clearing customs. Games started too late at Exhibition Stadium when rains were forecast. On and on it went. He had played to the hilt the role of the disgruntled player, eager to be traded elsewhere. Two years before Alexander had been the toast of the town beating the Yankees in the

AL East clinching game and being carried off the field by players and fans alike. Season ticket holders didn't like to see one of their own turn on them. Now he'd bombed out in Atlanta and been added for the stretch run by the Tigers. The cost was heavy for the 'win now and damn the future' Tigers who gave up John Smoltz, one of the best starters in the game today.

Nelson Liriano singled against Alexander, stole second and scored on a single by George Bell. The score stayed that way until the ninth as Jim Clancy put up one zero after another.Then one of Saturday night's lingerers, Kirk Gibson, led off the ninth with a solo homer over the right field fence against Tom Henke. That homer brought back memories of Butch Wynegar and kept the Tigers alive. On the Gibson scale of dramatic homers, the blast would rank just behind the night in Game 1 of the 1988 World Series when he would limp out of the Dodger dugout and whack a two-run, game-winning homer off Dennis Eckersley.

In the 11th, Evans hit a solo homer off Jeff Musselman and the Jays came back to score when Jesse Barfield delivered a two-out, run-scoring single.

In the 12th, Gibson blooped a single which scored the lead run. This time the Jays couldn't mount a second comeback. After being oh-so-close to bumping their lead to 4-1/2 games, the Jays' lead was back down to 2-1/2.

The Blue Jays went quickly, dropping three straight in an "anti-climactic" series against Milwaukee — although to the players it certainly shouldn't have been, considering the import. Manager Tom Trebelhorn said he was trying to do Sparky Anderson, his mentor, a favor.

On Thursday the Jays were off, while the Tigers played their fourth and final game in Baltimore. Pat Gillick spent the day trying to acquire Darrell Porter from the Rangers for the three-game weekend series as a replacement for Whitt but was unsuccessful.

If you believe in omens, you had to know right off the Jays were in for a rough time in Detroit. Their charter from Pearson International Airport in Toronto to Windsor had just climbed into the skies when a loud bang was heard on the left side of the aircraft. A Canada goose had been sucked into one of the huge turbines.

The plane circled and returned to the terminal. As many miles as they travel in a year, ball players are still notoriously superstitious travelers. Many wanted to rent cars and drive to Detroit, but management said no.

As the group reboarded the plane, George Bell stopped a flight attendant and asked: "What's the meal? Cooked goose?" While the Jays were flying around in circles, the Tigers won the final game in Baltimore to cut the Jays' lead to a single game.

Two wins in Detroit would make Toronto the champs of the AL East. If the Tigers won twice there would be a Monday playoff. A three-game sweep by the Tigers would mean "O.K., Blue Jays, Let's Play Golf."

Doyle Alexander wore his yellow pullover sweater to Tiger Stadium on the chilly opening night. "The same one I wore two years ago at Exhibition Stadium, they'll remember it," said Alexander, who was going head-to-head with Jim Clancy.

Surprisingly, Manny Lee staked the Jays a 3-0 lead with a three-run homer off Alexander. But Alexander and the Tigers were hanging tough.

The Tigers scored twice in the third and two more in the fourth and that was all the scorekeepers wrote: a 4-3 Detroit win, thanks to two unearned runs. After 160 games, we had a flat-footed tie with both teams owning 96-64 records.

Saturday was perhaps the best pitched game of the seven-game Detroit-Toronto series, as Flanagan duelled Morris strike for strike, run for run and out for out. From the fifth inning on manager Jimy Williams had a reliever warmed and ready to enter the game. Flanagan was one hit or a walk away from being removed. The Tigers could never manage the knock-out blow. Morris left after nine innings. Told by Williams he'd had enough after 12 innings, Flanagan said dryly: "Sorry I couldn't hold 'em guys."

Instead of going to Henke, who had been up three times when the Jays threatened, Williams went to lefty Jeff Musselman for the 13th. He walked Kirk Gibson to load the bases and Allan Trammell slashed a game-winning single through the legs of Lee to give the Tigers a 3-2 lead and put them up by a game.

Williams reasoned he wasn't going to use Henke in a game with the score tied, but what about tied pennant races? "What if I use him for two innings and then I have to use him another inning Sunday? I wouldn't have been able to use him Monday."

Monday never came for the Blue Jays. Jimmy Key faced Frank Tanana on Sunday, with the wind blowing out. Larry Herndon lofted a high fly to left field in the second. Off the bat Key thought it was "just another fly ball." So did George Bell in left. Except the ball continued to carry and carry, past the auxiliary scoreboard to land in the fourth row of seats.

The closest the Jays came to scoring was on a boloxed hit-and-run sign. With Cecil Fielder on first, third base coach John McLaren flashed the sign. Yet when Lee didn't see it, McLaren went to a signal which erased the previous sign. Except Fielder didn't see that cancellation.

So both the runner *and* the batter missed a sign. With Lee not swinging it became a straight steal and Fielder was thrown out easily. Of course, as so often happens in the grand old game, the rest of Lee's at bat only made the mistakes worse. He tripled. Had Fielder paid attention he would have scored to tie the game. Or had Lee picked up the original sign it would have been a game-tying triple. Not so. Lee was stranded at third.

With the likes of Juan Beniquez and Rick Leach batting around Bell, instead of Fernandez and Whitt, the American League MVP didn't have much protection in the batting order. He also didn't have much patience as the Tiger pitchers, under Sparky Anderson's orders, threw Bell nothing but pitches out of the strike zone. After carrying the team for much of the season, he tried to carry his team-mates one step further when a walk would have been just as good and he failed.

Tanana continued to mow down the Jays and when he fielded Garth Iorg's roller and threw underhanded to first, the Tigers had won the AL East title on the final day, the final pitch of the season.

Bell finished with a .308 batting average, 47 homers and 134 RBIs and in November was voted the MVP, the first player for a Canadian team ever to win such an honor. He outpointed Trammell 332-311 and had 16 first-place votes, to the 12 Trammell received. In December at the winter meetings in Houston, Bell was presented with the Major League Player of the Year award by *The Sporting News*.

Yet there had been no trip to post-season. Bell said he would have gladly traded both trophies for a couple of wins against the Tigers.

Assistant general manager Gordon Ash remembers the long drive back from Detroit with Pat Gillick on the final day of the season.

"I've seen him angry before," said Ash, "but I've never seen him immediately react. His face gets red but he doesn't yell and he's never made a move that wasn't thought through and discussed."

By the time the car had reached Woodstock, west of Toronto, Gillick's focus was on the 1988 season.

"That one, the seven losses in a row, was the hardest to take," Gillick was to say years later. "We were up 3-1 against Kansas City in 1985 and we should have won. Oakland was superior to the club we had in 1989. I don't think Minnesota was the better club (in 1991)."

Every ball club has its skeletons, its crosses to bear. Never did a season weigh so heavily on the shoulders of the Blue Jay players as the 1987 Motor City Meltdown.

As one fan said a month after the painful conclusion to the season: "In many ways cheering for the Blue Jays is like being caught in a smoke-filled room," he said of the season's rollercoaster ride. "The room is beginning to fill with smoke. You're gasping and gasping for air ... but the window is shut when you finally find it. You tug and tug at the lock, finally you get the window lifted and you stick your head out the window and take long, deep breaths of fresh air.

"Just when you think you're O.K. along come the Blue Jays to slam the window down on the back of your neck."

That's how painful 1987 was for Blue Jays fans.

SEVENTH INNING

♦1. Jimy Williams left baseball briefly in the early seventies to go into business for himself. What did he do?

♦2. Why did cranky Orioles manager Earl Weaver play the Jays' 1986 home opener under protest?

♦3. During the spring of '86, Dave Stieb, Cliff Johnson and another Blue Jay appeared in a newspaper promotion for a series of "fire safety tips." Name the third Jay.

♦4. This Blue Jay led the major leagues in home runs in 1986, the only Jay to ever do so. Name him.

♦5. In 1986, these two Jays became the first in team history to win Gold Gloves. Name them.

♦6. The Jays have played two tie games in their history, both against Cleveland, the first in 1984, the second in 1986, with the statistics from each game entered into the official record of both clubs. In the latter instance, this enabled one Blue Jay player to appear in 163 games during the 1986 season — name this hard-working player.

♦7. The Jays have had players drafted by the NBA and NFL. Name the Jays infielder who was a fourth-round draft pick of the Calgary Flames in 1986.

♦8. What major league record for shortstops did Tony Fernandez break in 1986?

♦9. Who was the first Jays pitcher to lead the American League in ERA?

♦10. Who was the first pitcher to win 100 games in a Blue Jays uniform?

♦11. The Jays' 1987 home opener caused a great deal of controversy in the United States — why?

♦12. On April 9, 1987, the Jays lost 14-3 to the Cleveland Indians. The game marked the first time that two 300-game winners had appeared in the same game. Who were they?

♦13. The Blue Jays' longest winning streak ever came to an end on June 13, 1987, after 11 straight wins. The Orioles ended their own 10-game losing skein by resorting to unusual means to change their luck. What did they do?

♦14. When the Toronto Blue Jays acquired veteran pitcher Phil Niekro on August 9, 1987, it represented a first in his long career — what was it?

♦15. After one late season game at Exhibition Stadium in 1987, two bats were sent to the Baseball Hall of Fame in Cooperstown — one belonging to Ernie Whitt, the other to Fred McGriff. Why?

♦16. George Bell's 47 home runs in 1987 set a new major league record for Latinos, breaking the old mark of 46 set by this San Francisco Giant in 1961 — name him.

♦17. What happened to first baseman Willie Upshaw after the 1987 season?

◆18. What was the so-called "rabbit ball"?

◆19. In 1987, which Jays pitcher set a major league record for most appearances without a win?

◆20. Name the player who set the Jays' team record for home runs by a rookie in a single season, a feat he accomplished in 1987.

Answers begin on page 151.

THE FRONT OFFICE

CHAPTER SEVEN

Neither the date nor the year matters. For the scene was played out day after day after day at Exhibition Stadium when the Jays and its top triumvirate were in town.

It's, say, five hours before game time:

In one office sits Paul Beeston. His feet hang over the side of his desk. A cigar hangs out of the corner of his mouth. The phone is placed to his ear as he chortles loudly with another baseball executive. His socks aren't hanging low because, of course, he isn't wearing socks.

Down the hall in another office, beneath a depth chart containing the names of 180-odd players in the organization, from major league down the rookie league, sits Pat Gillick. The Tony Lama cowboy boots he's wearing are draped over the side of his desk as he begins to tease someone over the speaker phone.

A few doors down, just back from either a staff ball hockey game or a jogging session during lunch hour, sits Gordon Ash, under a large photo of former Prime Minister Pierre Elliott Trudeau. The phone is glued to his ear.

Baseball may be played between the white lines, but most of the business of baseball is conducted over the phone and the majority of the day-to-day operations of the Blue Jays is conducted by these three men.

Negotiating TV deals, gathering information on players — from major leaguers to minor leaguers to amateurs, so trades can be made and draft choices can be charted —

Jays GM Pat Gillick has built the most successful franchise in baseball, but must have been tempted to take the field himself at times.
photo: Shane Harvey/Toronto Sun

crunching salary numbers for salary arbitration, placing players on waivers and deciding whether to sign players to long-term contracts, are all as much a part of baseball as the product you see unveiled every night at 7:35.

Once the Jays front office consisted of Pete, Paul and Pat.

Peter Bavasi departed at the end of the 1981 season. Now Paul Beeston is president, Pat Gillick is the executive vice-president and Gord Ash holds the title of assistant general manager.

To begin our look at the Toronto Blue Jays' front office, let's start with the No. 1 man and the initial employee hired by the team.

Paul Beeston was manager of Coopers & Lybrand accounting firm in London and a tax expert when the 30-year-old walked into the now-defunct Lord Simcoe Hotel on May 10, 1976 to be interviewed by Jays chairman R. Howard Webster and Don McDougall of Labatt's. By the time the interview was over, the Blue Jays had their first employee: vice-president, administration.

"I was nervous going in," says Beeston. "I was obviously the luckiest man in the world. They were offering me the job, a great job. It was mine to foul up by saying something stupid. It was obvious they were good guys and it was going to be a great place to work. Uprooting my family and moving from London to Toronto wasn't a difficult decision."

Money may have been Beeston's background but it wasn't Bay Street which drew him to Toronto; rather, it was an involvement with sport.

"Mr. Webster was an impressive man and a great person to work for," Beeston says of the Montreal native who shunned the limelight. Webster and Peter Hardy, who took over from Bavasi as chief executive officer, remained very much in the background of this young franchise.

In New York, after Reggie Jackson wasn't retained, angry fans knew who to vent their frustration against, chanting "Steinbrenner sucks, Steinbrenner sucks!" By contrast, few Blue Jays fans had ever seen Webster, much less seen him interviewed on TV or posing for the cover of *Sports Illustrated*.

"A lot of people received credit for this organization's success over the years," says Beeston, "and Mr. Webster can't be overlooked. He had serious involvement forming our management philosophy and then left people alone to do their work."

Webster was chairman of the board until 1983. He came to Toronto for the American League Championship Series in 1985 and was prepared to go to the game but at the last minute stayed at his hotel room and watched the game on TV. Because of failing health, he never visited the SkyDome. He died August 20, 1990 at the age of 80. As a tribute to the man, the best player on each of the Jays' minor league teams is awarded the R. Howard Webster Award.

Beeston is one of 15 "Day Oners" still working for a stable organization in what is far from a stable business. The rest of the list of long-timers includes executive vice-president Pat Gillick, as well as vice-presidents Bobby Mattick and Al LaMacchia. Others include director of scouting Bob Engle; Canadian scouting director Bob Prentice; scouting supervisor Duane Larson; director of minor league operations Ken Carson; director of stadium and ticket operations George Holm; director of public relations Howard Starkman; employee compensation manager Catherine Elwood; assistant director and manager (field operations) Len Frejlich; executive administrative assistant Sue Cannell; manager (ticket vault services) Paul Goodyear and manager (Commerce Court Tickets) Barb Walker.

McDougall, one of the threesome who deserves the credit for bringing baseball to Toronto along with Herb Solway and Paul Godfrey, attended classes at the University of Western Ontario. So did Beeston.

McDougall's next door neighbor in London was Pete Fowler, a good friend of Beeston's.

"We'd sit around Fowler's pool or McDougall's tennis court drinking beer," Beeston remembers. "I was the trivia nut. I knew baseball, football, tennis, cricket. Any kind of sports."

While McDougall thought the World Series was played in Los Angeles every year, Beeston had been weaned on baseball and other sports by his father Frank.

Paul Beeston saw his first pro ball game in the late fifties at the War Memorial Stadium in Buffalo. His father took him to see a game when the visitors were the Toronto Maple Leafs. Luke Easter and Rocky Nelson were the stars of the day.

"Growing up I had a lot of favorites," says Beeston. "Mickey Mantle and Yogi Berra of the Yankees. Jackie Robinson, Carl Furillo and Sal Maglie of the Dodgers. Maglie had pitched in Welland. I liked them all, like the song says, Mickey, Willie and the Duke."

In later years he'd make summer trips from the family cottage near Sarnia to Briggs Stadium to see the Detroit Tigers play. And weekend trips to Detroit were popular among Western students. In all Beeston guesses he'd been to Tiger Stadium to see "100 games or so" before he became a baseball money man.

Beeston is a gregarious, outgoing sort, yet he pauses when asked his best quality.

"Probably my biggest weakness is that I'm not a detail guy," says Beeston. "My strength is to get along with people, to negotiate and to get the most out of the people I work with. I'd be silly to be sitting around doing someone else's job."

Beeston's trademark, besides his cigar, is his aversion to wearing socks unless he's dressed in a suit and headed to a business meeting. Or unless it's cold outside. The sock thing is now out of control. When Beeston's name was mentioned as a successor to ousted commissioner Fay Vincent, many thought: "If Beeston's interested, he'll be wearing socks."

"We used to go to Crystal Beach (near Fort Erie, Ont.)," Beeston remembers. "A lot of the kids from Buffalo wouldn't wear socks in their shoes. I picked it up from them."

There was some idle talk that if the Jays ever won a World Series, Beeston would stick to socks. Yet he'll sport the *sans* socks look as the Jays defend the World Series title this year. He'll be comfortable as always. Even though exiled Yankee owner George Steinbrenner sent Beeston a congratulatory present of 10 pairs of socks after the Jays beat the Braves.

"To me, the three greatest moments in the history of the Blue Jays were October 25 (1992) in Atlanta," expounds Beeston, who watched the sixth and final World Series game with hockey star Wayne Gretzky, "then it would be the second last day of the 1985 season when Doyle Alexander beat the Yankees. That will always be special. It wasn't like we beat Seattle. The schedule had been make up the year before and here we were playing the Yankees for the whole ball of wax on the final Saturday of the year. The Yankees were George Steinbrenner, Dave Winfield, Billy Martin and Rickey Henderson.

"And the third most important day in franchise history was Opening Day 1977."

Says Bavasi: "Paul should be congratulated for understanding the tempo of the community and not getting too deeply involved in the baseball end of it. The great sign about an organization is how many people from day one are still around. I go to the winter meetings and it's like old home week with all the familiar faces of people still with the Blue Jays."

As for Gillick, his name was suggested to Bavasi by Tal Smith, formerly of Houston, and by Bob Fontaine, who used to be with San Diego.

"Pat and I had never worked together. I hired him over the phone," says Bavasi. "I told him he'd have to move here from Atlanta. We weren't going to be like the Expos where the front office packed up and headed south as soon as the gates closed on the final home date of the season."

After Bavasi's initial contact with Gillick, who was then employed by the Yankees in player development, Don McDougall received a phone call from Yankee owner George Steinbrenner.

Steinbrenner was enraged. He demanded Bavasi be fired for tampering with Gillick, who was his "best baseball person and the finest evaluator of talent in the game."

McDougall phoned Bavasi and told him what had transpired. Bavasi wondered whether the shoe was going to drop. After all, Steinbrenner had been helpful in getting the

Jays in the door when they were granted an expansion franchise.

Bavasi remembers McDougall saying, "So it looks like you're in trouble with Steinbrenner, but you've impressed us. The only way we would have been upset with you, is if Steinbrenner had said Gillick wasn't any good and you were trying to hire him."

The two finalists for the job of building the ball club were John Claiborne of the Boston Red Sox and Gillick. Claiborne was a solid salesman, while Gillick was considered just as talented but stronger when it came to scouting players, although some thought him too shy.

"I'm going to hire Gillick," is the way McDougall recalls a phone call from Bavasi. McDougall asked Bavasi why. "Because I talked with Neil MacCarl of the Toronto *Star* and he thinks the best guy for the job is Gillick."

How is that for the power of the media?

Hired August 16, 1976, Gillick was away from home 290 days in the Jays' first year of operation, searching for and assessing talent.

Gillick has perhaps been best described as someone who walks around like a man in the desert holding a huge, imaginary bowl of water. As he moves, the liquid slowly laps the sides of the container. And if he stops on his "cruise" about the SkyDome to acknowledge a hello, he'll find his attention will be diverted and some of the valuable water will slosh over the side.

"Pat Gillick is a tough guy for the public to read," says Bavasi. "I used to have people come in my office and ask 'Why doesn't Pat Gillick like me? I said hello and he didn't answer.' The fact is he's so focussed that some days he appears aloof.

"I'd tell them he was thinking about something else. Probably something more important."

With an I.Q. over 160, Gillick is constantly asking the question the computer asks: "What next?" This from a man who doesn't have a computer in his office. His chief piece of automation is a vacuum cleaner. When the Jays moved into their new plush offices at SkyDome, he vacuumed his rug constantly.

Gillick has never met a phone he didn't like, can't pass a bank of pay phones in an airport terminal without stopping, drives while punching numbers into the car phone and hasn't found an American Airlines AeroPhone he can't work. And he never looks the numbers up. He has memorized more phone numbers than you'll find in the New York City directory.

Jays scout Gordon Lakey tells the story of walking on the back diamond at the Cal-State Northbridge complex where he was to see first baseman Jason Thompson, then an amateur.

A groundskeeper came up. "You Gordon Lakey?" He told Lakey he had a phone call in the grounds crew's hut three fields down. It was Gillick.

His nickname at the University of Southern California was Segap Wolley. Segap Wolley? Yellow Pages spelled backwards.

"I always thought that the phone was meant to be used as a means of communication, but somehow Pat got it different," jokes a former Jays employee. "He uses it as a weapon. He calls any time, day or night. Big news or no news."

Gillick can be described as slightly eccentric, yet his sense of humor is like his pitching career as a minor leaguer — left-handed.

After 6 p.m. on a day which begins with a six-mile jog at 7 a.m., you can never be sure how he'll answer the phone in his office. "Good afternoon ... World Champion Oakland Athletics."

In the past he's answered P.R. director Howard Starkman's line and had a CBS executive suddenly nervous when the TV type asked about parking privileges. Gillick told the New Yorker since CTV had the rights for the game, CBS wouldn't be allowed to bring its truck into the CNE grounds.

He's phoned a sportswriter with other writers listening on the speaker phone to tease him about how badly his Kentucky Derby pick fared.

A few years back the Jays filed an odd salary arbitration figure of $747,000 on shortstop Tony Fernandez. Why the 747 number he was asked? "We thought it would fly,"said

Gillick.

How does Gillick describe his sense of humor?
"What sense of humor?" he replies.

To be a GM one has to be heavy-handed. It's part of the job. An agent tells of a late-night pre-arbitration hearing where voices grew louder and louder until Gillick said, "Step outside." Cooler heads prevailed.

For all the bluster, he's a man of considerable sensitivity. During the '88 season he wept openly as Jeff Musselman explained his alcohol addiction and how he'd let down his parents. A standing ovation still sends a chill down Gillick's spine and his eyes will mist over. When DH Dave Parker was acquired for the stretch run in 1991, he received a lengthy ovation. Gillick dabbed his eyes, but had the tears cleared away in time to see Parker deliver an RBI double.

He's also the man who flew to Dallas from Toronto following the 1990 season to inform third base coach John McLaren face-to-face he wouldn't be back at the same position next year. Gillick wept openly as he tried to convince McLaren, a "Day Oner" and a former scout, to take another position in the organization.

He managed two hours sleep after dealing his favorite player Willie Upshaw to the Indians in the spring of 1988. Upshaw had been the foundation of the franchise, being selected in the major league draft. If Upshaw had been a gigantic flop, who knows how long it would have taken the Jays to contend?

After Upshaw came George Bell, Jim Gott, Jim Acker, Kelly Gruber, Manuel Lee and on and on. Each one gave the Jays the chance to improve quicker while their expansion cousins, the Mariners, stood by the June amateur draft as a means of improving.

Gillick grew up wanting to be an FBI agent. And some of his escapades, whether it be chasing free-agent reliever Goose Gossage in San Diego or free-agent right-hander Jose Pett last year in Sao Paulo, Brazil, tend to be clandestine.

"Development has always been his passion," says Ash. "He always asks me why there aren't more black hockey players. He wants to know why there aren't any baseball players from Africa or Russia."

He's still on the road over 150 days a year and although Bob Engle is the scouting director, Gillick keeps his hand in. He flew to Washington state nine times during the summer of 1989 in an attempt to sign third-round pick John Olerud. Each year he concentrates on a few special projects, difficult signs. He signed shortstop Alex Gonzalez in 1991, but was unsuccessful in luring Shea Morenez out of the University of Texas quarterback huddle.

"His best quality?" says good friend Beeston. "It's his brain power. His dedication. His knowledge of baseball. He's the most remarkable of all GMs. He has a tireless ability to deal with inane questions from reporters."

Peter Hardy, David Lewis, John Robarts, Howard Webster and McDougall formed the first Blue Jays board of directors. New to the business, they were extremely patient and for the most part didn't interfere. Ocassionally, however...

"When a board member used to ask what I call a 'why question,' as in 'Why is this player up and this guy still in Syracuse?' or 'Why didn't we sign this guy?' it was very upsetting to Gillick," says Bavasi. "I learned very early you can't ask scouting people why. It's the wrong question. They have a sixth, seventh, eighth or ninth sense that gives them the confidence to take a leap of faith. It's difficult for business people to understand."

Bavasi learned his lesson early about interfering. He told Gillick during spring training not to pull the trigger on a deal which would have sent scheduled Opening Day starter Bill Singer to the Yankees for a young lefty, Ron Guidry.

For the record, Singer, the ex-Dodger and two-time 20-game winner, went 2-8, with a 6.79 ERA, and didn't win a game after May. Guidry won the Cy Young award in 1978, going 25-3, and won 170 career games for the Yankees.

"Gillick is the finest player personnel director in the business," says Bavasi. "His ego is moderate to very low."

Gillick had an early introduction to Canada. In 1956 he played summer ball for the Granum White Sox outside of Fort McLeod, Alta. "I wasn't sure where it was," says Gillick. "They said go all the way to Great Falls, change buses and then go across the border at Coutts and the next thing you're in Lethbridge and the people from the club will pick you up there."

The dean of baseball general managers says the 1995 will be his final season. Gillick wants to learn to fly, to sail and maybe to ski when he retires. "And in my spare time I'll harass sportswriters by phone," he jokes.

While Beeston is a money man and Gillick is a baseball man, Gordon Ash is a money man heading in the other direction. He was interviewed by San Diego before the Padres lured away the Mets' No. 1 man, Joe McIlvaine, and his name came up when the Florida Marlins went looking for a GM. He's respected among his peers, not to mention agents. The second task is a lot more difficult than the first.

Ash is considered the heir apparent to Gillick's job when he retires.

It has been a strange road to the top. Prior to joining the Jays, his nuts-and-bolts baseball background was limited to working with the grounds crew at Exhibition Stadium.

Ash took history at York University and hoped to land a teaching job. However, "about the only jobs open were in Moosonee and I knew that wasn't for me," he says. He landed in the Canadian Imperial Bank of Commerce's management trainee program. While working at the bank and moving from branch to branch were stimulating at first, Ash eventually tired of his job. He had a friend working as a part-timer in the Blue Jays ticket office that first April. Besides earning extra money, ticket sellers were able to see a few innings for free once the windows were closed.

"That's what interested me the most," Ash remembers. "I went down and applied and started working part-time for the Jays Victoria Day 1977."

On February 1, 1978, George Holm, the director of ticket operating, hired Ash full time. He accepted less money than he was making at the CIBC. "It was funny. I was running away from the bank because I wanted some variety in my working life. With the Blue Jays, I was working in mail-order tickets. After about two weeks of that, the excitement began to wear off."

In 1979, Ash moved from the ticket office to become operations supervisor. The job included everything from groundskeeping to helping roll out the tarp. Elliott Wahle, administrator of player personnel, left to join Toys R Us in 1983 and a year later, Ash was named his successor.

While releasing a player still causes Gillick sleepless nights, Ash says he wasn't bothered by the task during during spring training when he ran the minor-league department. "By releasing some players we're doing them a favor; it's time they got on with the rest of their lives," says Ash. "I've released players who are successful in the business world and come back and tell me. Mind you, they don't agree with it at the time."

Nowadays, he has to be less than charitable than he was as a youngster working for the Salvation Army. "In this job you have to keep in mind that every settlement impacts subsequent settlements," he says. "Each contract sets a precedent that will be thrown back at you the next time around."

Contract negotiations can be very bitter, as he discovered early on with player agent Craig Fenech over Tom Henke's 1987 contract. Henke stormed out of training camp and called Ash a "liar."

"I was a novice and Tom was a novice, neither of us had control over the situation," says Ash.

Ash's tale is an only-in-America story, which happened in Canada. "The Blue Jays took a chance on me and let me learn at my own speed," says Ash. "The good thing about this organization is that it gives you the freedom to make your own decisions. You dive into your job and hopefully you're able to swim. Whenever you sink to the bottom of the pool there's somebody there to help you out."

It was Ash who equipped all Jays scouts and minor league managers with lap-top computers. At his suggestion the club has begun to compile a video library of every player in the organization.

"Paul Beeston always says he's the luckiest guy in the world," says Ash. "I guess I'm the second luckiest. When I was young I wasn't so sure why I was so attracted to baseball but now I look back and I think I was drawn to tradition, the sense or order and history."

"Our Americans beat their Americans," is the way one newscaster termed the Blue Jays' World Series victory over the Atlanta Braves.

Well, they aren't all Americans. Ash isn't and neither is Beeston. Nor are Herb Solway and Don McDougall, who helped bring the team here.

"We would have given our fans a better team earlier if the sale of the Giants had gone through," says Solway, "but it we had bought the Giants, I don't think we would have been able to hire bright young people like Paul Beeston and Pat Gillick. We probably would have retained the people who worked for the Giants. Fans would have seen the Giants playing, say, .480 ball. With an expansion franchise the whole thing has been built on a natural progression."

What a long journey it has been.

"Winning the World Series was a wonderful feeling," says Solway, now on the board of directors, "but the feeling wasn't as exciting as the day we were finally granted the expansion franchise in 1976."

McDougall credits Bavasi and his marketing for the club's early success.

Looking back, the first Blue Jay executive is quite reflective. "I tried to do too much," says Bavasi. "I was going like a house on fire. I was too hard on people. I think Peter Hardy (vice-chairman of the Jays board of directors) sensed that and wouldn't support me in that weakened condition." According to Bavasi, in November 1981 Hardy told him "it was time to retire."

For three years Bavasi worked as a consultant in Tampa. At one time he had 21 clients including expansion franchise aspirants in Buffalo and St. Petersburg plus broadcasting deals with the Royals and the Yankees and a spring training consultancy with the Astros.

"Baseball is a game of redemption," says Bavasi. "A pitcher goes 1-1/3 innings and he's pulled, and then the next start he throws a shutout. Or a hitter strikes out in the seventh inning with the bases loaded and hits a game-winning home run in the ninth.

"I needed redemption. The ball team might have been a success at the gate, but I didn't manage either Gillick or Beeston very well. I wish now, looking back on it, that I'd been older and more mature."

Iin 1984, he joined the sad-sack Cleveland Indians seeking redemption. "You can't redeem yourself with a good franchise...I didn't need to go to Cleveland, but I went and in 1986 we made money for the first time in 30 years and we drew 1.5 million in attendance, the highest in 27 years."

The night the Jays won the World Series, Don McDougall remembers thinking back to Day One.

"It may be bad to say so, but at the time we started with this team, we thought only Americans could run a baseball team," he says. "There was a great satisfaction being in Atlanta seeing the team win and seeing 'Day One' people like Paul Beeston, Pat Gillick, George Holm and Howard Starkman. They were all the people who make the business work.

"There's no question the architect of the team has been Pat Gillick, and Paul Beeston has worked the business side successfully to the point where the franchise is the envy of almost every owner in baseball."

EIGHTH INNING

◆1. What notable trade did the Jays' Pat Gillick pull in 1988?

◆2. What was unusual about George Bell's Opening Day performance in 1988?

◆3. What was most noteworthy about the Jays' 1988 home opener against the New York Yankees?

◆4. On three occasions in his career, Dave Stieb has taken a no-hitter to the final out, only to have it broken up with an untimely hit. Two of them were back to back, in September 1988. Was that the first time any pitcher had thrown consecutive one-hitters?

◆5. Name the two batters who ruined those afternoons for Stieb in September '88.

◆6. Jays' manager Jimy Williams spent a lot of time trying to get George Bell out of left field to become a full-time DH in '88, and Bell's team record error binge in left gave credence to Williams' cause. How many errors did Bell make: a) 10 b) 15 c) 25 d) 50?

◆7. On July 17, 1989, Tom Henke saved both ends of a doubleheader against the California Angels, the second time he'd accomplished the feat. The same day, this pitcher won both games — who was he?

◆8. This Blue Jay, signed as a free agent in '88, once made a record four errors in one game as a third baseman. Name him.

◆9. The first and only Blue Jay to hit for cycle managed the feat on April 16, 1989. Who was it?

◆10. Name the Blue Jay who broke up two no-hitters in the ninth inning, within a five-day span in 1989.

◆11. During the '89 season, Cito Gaston became the fourth black manager in Major League Baseball history. Name the first three.

◆12. What's Cito Gaston's actual given name?

◆13. What's Mookie Wilson's actual given name?

◆14. When Junior Felix stepped to the plate for the first time on May 4, 1989, what major-league record was he about to tie?

◆15. On June 2, 1989, this Blue Jay became the first player to hit an inside-the-ballpark grand slam since Mel Stottlemyre did it for the Yankees on July 20, 1965. Who was he?

◆16. Did the Jays leave Exhibition Stadium with an all-time winning record at home?

◆17. Who was the only man to appear in uniform at both the Jays' Opening Day in 1977 at Exhibition Stadium and the SkyDome opener in 1989?

◆18. Who was the first man up to bat when the Jays made their SkyDome opener on June 5, 1989?

◆19. Why is SkyDome the only major league ballpark with foul chains, as opposed to foul poles?

◆20. There was a lot of interest in what effect playing in the new SkyDome would have on the Jays. With the roof open, the Jays were 22-20 over the balance of the 1989 regular season. How many games did they lose with the lid closed?

◆21. This utility infielder, who played for the Jays in 1989 and '90, was the only man ever traded for Pete Rose — name him.

◆22. In early August 1989, the Jays landed two experienced players from the New York Mets. One of them was Mookie Wilson — who was the other?

◆23. Who was the first Blue Jays player to make a cameo appearance on *Sesame Street*?

◆24. On September 23, 1989, which Blue Jay forgot his place in the batting order and sat out a round?

◆25. Which player set a league championship series record for steals, against the Jays in the 1989 ALCS?

Answers begin on page 153.

You could say Rick Bosetti was a whiz in the outfield.
photo: Barry Gray/Toronto Sun

STRANGE DAYS, STRANGE JAYS
CHAPTER EIGHT

First off, as you should know by now, *all* major league ball players are a little strange.

And, over the course of 16 seasons, a few things out of the ordinary are bound to happen. More often than not, offbeat players are the featured perfomers in most of the interesting tales in Jays lore.

Take Tim Johnson, for instance. He was a regular fixture with the Milwaukee Brewers at shortstop until a player named Robin Yount arrived on the scene. With the Blue Jays he was strictly a back-up. He played 70 games (only 82 at bats) in 1978 behind Luis Gomez and 43 games (86 at bats) backing up American League Rookie of the Year Alfredo Griffin and Danny Ainge in 1979 at the infield spots.

However, there was one occasion that Johnson played three straight days at shortstop because of an injury to Griffin. Johnson wasn't used to this heavy workload. By the fourth day he'd had enough. He walked into manager Roy Hartsfield's office, slammed his fist on the desk and yelled, "Sit me or trade me!"

Today, Johnson is proud of his Blue Jay heritage.

"I wore the uniform when it was nothing, when we lost 100 games a year. Now I'm proud to watch them on the TV and say 'Hey, I played for that team once,'" he says. In fact, when the Montreal Expo advance scout is feeling melancholy, he heads to the only bar in Indianapolis which sells Labatt's beer, pulls up a stool, watches the game on the TV and thinks about rooming with Bob Bailor at the Seaway Hotel.

The since-demolished Seaway Hotel was once home-away-from-home for many of the players away from home. They'd check out for a lengthy road trip — there wasn't any staying in the SkyDome Hotel or the equivalent in those days — and check back in on their return.

One such morning a giddy group was checking in after an all-night truly red-eye flight back from the west coast. Coach Harry Warner told the new desk clerk he wanted and needed a room "on the gulf side."

The desk clerk was trying to be civil to his guests. "I'm sorry sir, that is not a gulf out there, that's Lake Ontario," he said.

Warner looked at him quizzically and said loudly: "I don't mean the lake. I want to be on the side of the Gulf gas station. If you put us up against the Gardiner Expressway no one will get any sleep because of the traffic."

Warner wasn't the only coach with a sense of humor. Billy Smith coached first base for five years. "Turn left, turn left!" Smith would yell in his high-pitched voice with the North Carolina twang.

One could make a case for Smith as the most successful manager, inning for inning, in franchise history. On July 20, 1984 the Jays were playing their expansion cousins in Seattle's Kingdome. Losing 3-1, the Jays weren't in a good mood and it turned worse, especially when Jimmy Key was charged with a balk in the seventh inning.

Manager Bobby Cox was ejected after launching a vigorous protest. Third base coach Jimy Williams took over, chipped in with his two cents and he too was ejected. Then pitching coach Al Widmar passed on a few choice words and he got the thumb, making it a threesome huddling in the hallway leading to the clubhouse, watching the Jays' outs dwindle down to a precious few.

That left Smith in charge for the rest of the way. Three outs away from losing, Billy's boys scored 11 times. With the Jays' bullpen in those days, the 12-3 lead was just about enough. Even though Seattle managed four runs in the home half of the ninth, Toronto and skipper Smith wound up with a 12-7 victory.

Someone who had as many victories as Smith, but far more opportunities, was right-hander Mark Lemongello who came over from the Astros in a 1979 deal. He was a tad different, and it's fair to say he didn't see playing in a new country as the wonderful adventure other players did. "Being traded to Toronto freaked him out," remembers Bob Bailor. "His line used to be 'I'm not playing in any foreign country.' He threw right-handed but he thought left-handed."

Lemongello didn't pitch in Canada that long.

Peter Bavasi, Pat Gillick, and minor league director Elliott Whale called in Lemongello to tell him that he, his 1-9 record and 6.29 ERA were headed to Triple-A Syracuse. Lemongello picked up an ashtray and fired it at Gillick. Like most of his throws directed at the strike zone, he missed, but the ashtray put a major league dent in the glass wall of the boardroom.

The three Jays executives came scurrying out of the office as if someone had dropped free draft picks on the floor. Lemongello stormed past the secretaries and headed to the clubhouse.

Lemongello, of course, wasn't the only one to throw a temper tantrum.

Second baseman Damo Garcia, upset over an error and his position in the batting order during the 1986 season, took to the showers after a bad loss in Oakland one night and burned his uniform. All that succeeded in doing was to to burn his bridges with Williams.

Danny Ainge, class of 1979-81, made a brief stay in Toronto before going on to basketball.

"I can remember watching him in the outfield when I was with Milwaukee sitting in the bullpen," says Buck Martinez. "He'd stand there and in between pitches he'd smooth the grass out with his cleats. Like he was evening out the dirt as if he was playing the infield. In some ways he was like George Brett. Everything he did he did with an enthusiasm not many major leaguers had. He was fresh. It was like he was straight out of Little League."

Ainge was a right-handed hitter. Except for one game in Texas when he suddenly stepped to the plate and batted left-handed against right-hander Doc Medich.

"He went 2-for-3 and if you added up the two hits, they wouldn't have travelled a total of 20 feet," says Garth Iorg.

Yet the strangest of the strange had to be centre fielder Rick Bosetti, who used to think it was fun to urinate on the field during a pitching change.

"He'd announce on the bench he was going to do it when we went out in the next half inning," says Iorg. "Somehow he'd get his zipper down. He'd hold his glove below the waist facing down and if you looked close enough this stream would be coming out.

"It wasn't very noticeable. The last person anyone watches during a pitching change was the centre fielder. Everyone looks at the manager, the pitcher who's leaving or the new pitcher."

Bosetti was the Jays' centre fielder for three years, but to start the 1981 season the Jays' anointed No. 1 draft, Lloyd Moseby, was the new man in the middle.

"The Jays were 100 per cent right in what they did, Lloyd had a great career. But Bosetti didn't like the fact that there wasn't any competition for the job," remembers Iorg. "We opened in Detroit and Bosetti said he'd made up his mind: (Manager) Bobby Mattick was going to see him every time he turned around."

Mattick would get out of his seat and turn and there would be Bosetti standing in his way. Sometimes the benched centre fielder would sit in Mattick's seat. That went on all of Opening Day in Detroit and for a couple of innings during the second game of the season, until, "Bobby turned and bumped into Bosetti again," laughs Iorg. "Bobby screamed: 'BOSETTI! GET TO THE BULLPEN!'"

The Jays' original manager, Roy Hartsfield, called 'Dandruff' by the umpires, also had difficulties handling Bosetti. He worked through an intermediary, left-handed starter Tom Underwood.

"Roy would never have Bo into the office by himself," recalls Underwood. "He thought Bo was a little crazy. So every time Bo did something that Roy didn't like, he'd shake his head, turn to me and say 'Undie, get your boy and bring him in.'"

Aside from whizzing on the artificial turf, missed cutoff throws, missed signs and the frustration of the 100-loss seasons would earn Bosetti a special audience.

Wild nights are, of course, a staple of baseball lore. But times have changed since the Jays' early days.

"Back then ball players would get into a row and you could pay off the barkeep for the damages and that was the end of it," says Bosetti. "Now you end up on the front page or in rehab. It was just players blowing off the stress and strain of playing 162 games a year."

Luis Leal was never accused of staying out late. Only of eating too much.

During one Saturday game in 1985, he lasted less than two innings on the mound. Back in the clubhouse, a six-foot-long sandwich, supplied by Mr. Submarine as part of a promotion, awaited. Normally, players would eat the sandwich after the game. This afternoon, however, Leal got a head start, causing some to suspect he'd bowed out early intentionally.

In the course of telling and re-telling the Leal story over the years, the tale has gone from Leal having eaten just a few bites of the sub to devoring fully half of the six-footer. Another few years they'll tell the story and only crumbs will be left on the table.

Leal wasn't the only pitcher to struggle during those formative years. Buck Martinez told Jim Gott that the way to get out former team-mate Gorman Thomas was to throw breaking balls away and crowd him inside with the hard stuff, especially late in the count.

"It gets to 3-2 and I call for a fastball and I'm going to set up inside," remembers Martinez of Gott's abbreviated stay as a reliever. "He shakes me off once, then a second time. He wants to throw a slider away, so I nod. He throws it and Thomas hits a home run to win the game. I look at him afterwards and he says 'I know, I know.'"

A week later the Brewers played the Jays again. Gott was on the mound trying to protect a lead and Thomas was the hitter.

"I call a fastball inside and he shakes me off again," says Martinez. "So out I go and Gott says 'He can't possibly be looking for a slider.' He hit it a ton for a home run."

Tommy Hutton, now a Blue Jays broadcaster, was a part-time player with the Jays. Since he had a lounge act as a singing guitarist in the off-season, he was also a part-time musician deep in the bowels of Exhibition Stadium.

In 1978, Hutton formed the Blue Jays Blues Band with Hutton singing and playing bass guitar, while right-hander Jim Clancy played guitar and boss man Peter Bavasi sat in on drums. Chuck Berry classics and other rock 'n' roll hits dominated their repertoire.

Bavasi and Pat Gillick later sold Hutton's contract to the Expos, in a stretch run at the time, for $35,000 and a player to be named.

"I went back down the next day to where we played and Clancy came up to me," recalls Bavasi. "He said: 'You have to be the dumbest general manager I've ever played for. You trade Hutton and you don't even get a bass player in return.'"

One year, long before agents dominated the scene, Bavasi and Clancy got down to the wire on contract negotiations, with the right-hander handling his own contract talks. Clancy wouldn't sign, so Bavasi came up with the answer that turned the tables.

Bavasi told Clancy that if he would agree to sign for the amount the Jays were offering, Bavasi would buy him a brand new electric guitar and a brand new amplifier from a music store in Etobicoke.

Clancy had two questions when he walked into the store. The first: "What's the most expensive guitar you have?" A Les Paul model for $800. The second: "What's your most expensive amplifier?" It was worth $1,200.

Bavasi shrugged: "It would have been cheaper if I'd given him what he wanted."

Bavasi's strength was promotion which wasn't lost on Tommy Underwood.

"I started off the 1979 season at 0-9, but Roy Hartsfield respected me and he kept giving me the ball," recalls Underwood. "I lost the seventh game of that streak to my brother Pat and that really pissed me off. It was my brother's first game. He phoned me Friday and said the Tigers had called him up, which was great news.

"He hadn't pitched in the big leagues before, but I didn't figure he'd get a chance to pitch that quick."

Detroit was coming to Exhibition Stadium for a four-game series and Tommy Underwood was scheduled to pitch the fourth game on Thursday. The lefty picked up his brother Pat at the airport and he said: "I'm pitching the fourth game."

"That upset me, really pissed me off," says Underwood. "I figured it was some propaganda thing. I mean, here he is, he's never pitched in the majors and he just happens to be starting against me."

Down the hall marched Underwood to visit Bavasi.

"Bavasi swore he had nothing to do with it, he looked sincere," Underwood remembers, "but you know Bavasi, so I looked at him and said, 'If you have nothing to do with it, prove it by flying up my whole family first class to watch.' He did. Although I'd convinced my dad it was just a propaganda thing, he didn't come. I think he regrets it now."

Underwood vs. Underwood was a great match up, despite the pre-game disgust and distraction, much like when the Niekro brothers, Joe and Phil, first hooked up against each other.

The game was scoreless until the eighth. Jerry Morales hit a lead-off homer in the eighth and the Tigers had a 1-0 lead. Pat went 8-1/3 innings, allowing three hits to combine with Dave Tobik and Scarboro's John Hiller for the shutout.

"It was the only shutout my brother ever threw," says Underwood. "The game was on TV back in Detroit and they hadn't come back from the commercials when Morales hit the home run, so the TV came back and all people saw was the guy rounding second. So there was only one run in the ball game and no one in America saw the ball hit."

Unlike Lemongello, Underwood didn't continue to sink into oblivion. He rebounded after his 0-9 start and finished 9-16 to lead the club in wins that year.

In the course of 16 seasons there have been nights when pitchers like Leal, Gott, Lemongello and Underwood couldn't get it done. On those occasions the Jays would turn to position players for an inning or two. First baseman Craig

Kusick pitched four innings in 1979, outfielder Bob Bailor worked two innings over three games in 1980 and outfielder Rick Leach pitched an inning in 1984.

Faced with a thin or tired bullpen and a lost cause, the manager would turn to a former high school pitcher or anyone with a live arm. The first non-pitcher to take the mound at Exhibition Stadium, however, pitched for the Orioles.

In the midst of a 24-10 loss to the Jays on June 26, 1978, Earl Weaver brought on Larry Harlow and after he was rocked, turned to catcher Elrod Hendricks. Of course, the sight of Hendricks throwing change-ups was a laughing matter to those on the Orioles bench, at least those who couldn't be seen by Weaver.

Bavasi wasn't laughing. He was outraged. He tried to reach the president of the American League to register a protest, claiming Weaver was making a travesty of the game.

On August 25, 1979, down 22-2 in the sixth inning against the Angels, Roy Hartsfield gave the ball to Craig Kusick. He couldn't have fared worse than those who were paid to pitch. They'd given up 26 hits 13 for extra bases, including five homers.

As Kusick headed for the mound, utility man Tim Johnson tried to get Hartsfield's attention. "Timmy wanted to come in as my catcher, the way Steve Carlton had Tim McCarver as his regular catcher," said Kusick.

Kusick, who had pitched in college, put on quite a show. He doffed his hat to the crowd and then did an impression of Kansas City's Al (The Mad Hungarian) Hrabosky, storming around the mound, slamming his fist into his glove, pausing for meditation and charging onto the mound to face the first batter. His delivery was like Luis Tiant's twisting style.

Kusick allowed two earned runs on three hits and didn't walk a man. He induced Don Baylor, who already had a team-record eight RBIs thanks to a grand slam, into popping up twice.

He did give up a two-run homer but later blamed his defence. "Al Woods should have jumped into the stands for that one," said Kusick, who said he threw an "outstanding sinker, curve and some stuff from Laredo."

Former umpire Marty Springstead worked Exhibition Stadium often before moving to the front office. Today, he's the American League's supervisor of officials. While the Jays certainly had their share of oddball players, Springstead says the paying customers were a little off the wall themselves.

"The fans were somewhat strange, like a hockey crowd," he remembers. "The seats were so close you could hear everything the fans yelled at you. One time a guy yelled 'Why don't you retire and give a kid who can see a chance?' and another time some guy yelled 'You always spend your holidays up here?'"

Springstead remembers Exhibition Stadium not for seagulls or fans but for a forfeiture. Earl Weaver's Orioles were playing in the rain at Exhibition Stadium and were losing 5-0 in the fifth to Jim Clancy.

The Orioles left fielder slipped on the small tarp which covered the left field bullpen chasing a foul ball.

"Weaver comes out and he wants us to take the tarps off both bullpens or he's not playing," says Springstead. "Larry Barnett and I told him we couldn't do that because they'd be a mess for the relievers if they had to warm up in the eighth or ninth.

"Anyways I made a compromise and for the life of me I don't know why I did it. But we removed the cinder blocks and only covered one side of the bullpen mound. He still wouldn't play. So the Orioles walked off the field and we awarded the game to Toronto by a 9-0 score. In those years a five-run lead wasn't that safe. Baltimore was still in the race, too."

The fact Weaver would rather pack up and head home with a race on in the AL East was strange.

And, for that night, the strangest man in the park wasn't wearing a Toronto uniform.

NINTH INNING

♦1. Name the Blue Jay who is the first player in major league history to have three consecutive 100 RBI seasons with three different teams.

♦2. Who was the catcher for Dave Stieb's no-hitter against Cleveland on September 2, 1990?

♦3. What was unusual about the Toronto Blue Jays' 1991 schedule, the year they won their second AL East championship?

♦4. In 1992, Pat Borders led the American League in appearances as a catcher with 136. In doing so, he also tied a team record — with who?

♦5. What record did pitcher Jack Morris set in the Jays' first game of the 1992 season?

♦6. In 1992, the Blue Jays signed the first Brazilian to a major league baseball contract, for a club record $500,000 signing bonus — name him.

♦7. At the time he was traded to the Jays in August '92, pitcher David Cone was on his way to becoming the first National League pitcher since Warren Spahn (1949-51) to lead the league in strikeouts three years in a row. But he was edged out 215-214 at season's end by a pitcher he would later face in the World

Series – name him.

♦8. What AL record was set, and major-league record tied, after the Jays' 22-2 defeat at the hands of the Milwaukee Brewers on August 28, 1992?

♦9. In Game 4 of the 1992 ALCS, the Jays staged the biggest comeback in AL playoff history — how many runs behind were they before they rallied?

♦10. Which Blue Jay was selected Most Valuable Player in the 1992 ALCS?

♦11. This former Jay made only three appearances in his brief career in Toronto, but in 1992, while playing for Atlanta, he came off the bench and delivered the winning run in the Braves' heart-stopping victory in Game 7 of the NLCS. Name him.

♦12. What was Jack Morris' post-season record in 1992?

♦13. During the 1988 World Series, Kirk Gibson became the first pinch-hitter in series history to hit a home run in the ninth inning to bring his team from behind to win. In 1992, which Blue Jay became the second?

♦14. During Game 3 of the 1992 World Series, the Blue Jays came within an eyelash of pulling off the first triple play in 72 years of World Series play, when Kelly Gruber dove to tag out this player called safe at second — name him.

♦15. Which Atlanta Brave belted a grand slam off Jack Morris in Game 5 of the 1992 World Series, putting an end to the Jays' aspirations of winning the Series at home?

♦16. During the 1992 World Series, Atlanta set a record for bases stolen in a six-game series with 14. How many baserunners did Jays catcher Pat Borders throw out?

◆17. What post-season batting record did World Series MVP Pat Borders set in 1992?

◆18. Which Blue Jay tied Tony Kubek and Willie McCovey's record for most positions started in World Series play?

◆19. Kelly Gruber's 0-23 hitless streak in post-season play broke the old record of hitting futility held by two players, one of whom was a team-mate of his. Name him.

◆20. Which pitcher got credit for the win in the World Series finale?

Answers begin on page 156.

THE BEST (AND WORST) OF THE JAYS
CHAPTER NINE

Ten biggest plays in Blue Jay history

1. DH Dave Winfield hits 11th-inning double, October 24, 1992.

With two out and the score tied 2-2 in the top of the 11th, he pulls a pitch inside the third base line to score Devon White and Robbie Alomar, supplying the winning run in the final game of the 1992 World Series.

2. CF Devon White makes catch, chest against the centre field wall, October 20, 1992.

With Terry Pendleton on first and Deion Sanders on second in Game 3 of the World Series, David Justice lines a Juan Guzman pitch to straightaway centre which White flags down as he crashes into the centre field fence. Pendleton is called out for passing Sanders on the base paths and Kelly Gruber appears to tag Sanders on the foot as he retreats to second. Second base ump Bob Davidson calls Sanders safe but the next day, after looking at pictures, admitted he'd made a mistake, cancelling what would have been a triple play.

3. C Buck Martinez is out for the season after making a rare double play at home plate, July 10, 1985, Seattle.

M's Phil Bradley is on second when Gorman Thomas singles to right. Jesse Barfield throws home. Bradley crushes Martinez, ripping the ligaments in the catcher's ankle and twisting his leg. Thomas runs to second on the throw and now heads for third. Martinez tries to throw and sails the ball into left. George Bell throws home and Martinez

Dave Winfield belts the 11th inning double in Game 6 of the 1992 World Series, driving in the margin of victory.
photo: Stan Behal/Toronto Sun

catches it in time to tag Thomas. Your ordinary 9-2-7-2 double play.

4. *OF Joe Carter's singles off Angels' Bryan Harvey, October 2, 1991.*

Down a run in the bottom of the ninth, Devon White leads off with a single. White goes all the way around to score and Robbie Alomar winds up on second when Kevin Flora fields Alomar's grounder and trying for the force at second, throws the ball into left field. Alomar steals third on the next pitch and scores on Carter's game-winning hit through a drawn-in infield for a 6-5 win to give the Jays the AL East title.

5. *LF George Bell hits scoring fly ball off RP Mark Williamson, September 30, 1989.*

Mookie Wilson tags and scores to cap three-run rally for a 4-3 win over Baltimore at SkyDome to eliminate the Orioles and give the Jays the AL East.

6. *2B Robbie Alomar's two-run homer off Dennis Eckersley to tie the score in Game 4 of the ALCS, October 10, 1992.*

Jays win in extra innings to turn the series in their favor and take the ALCS in six games.

7. *DH Dave Winfield grand slam, May 7, 1992.*

Down three runs in the top of the ninth inning, Winfield turns around a Mike Schooler pitch for a two-out, grand slam homer and a 10-9 victory.

8. *Triple play, September 21, 1979.*

The Jays pulled a fast one on the Yankees for help in a 3-2 win. With lefty Tom Underwood pitching for the Jays, Chris Chambliss is on first and Roy Staiger on second. Damaso Garcia, then with the Yankees, hits a line drive to Jays second baseman Dave McKay. McKay catches the liner and fires to first baseman Craig Kusick for the second out and he throws on to second to Alfredo Griffin to catch Chambliss for the third out.

9. *Doug Ault hits the first of two homers, April 7, 1977.*

Ault wakes up the snowbirds with a homer off Ken Brett to warm the excited 44,649 first-timers.

10. *DH George Bell has three homer day against Bret Saberhagen, Opening Day, April 4, 1988.*

After a spring of frustration over whether he would assume DH duties or not, Bell goes deep three times en route to a 5-3 victory in Kansas City.

Five best pitched games

1. *Dave Stieb vs. the Indians, September 2, 1990.*
(A no-hitter!)
After many a near miss, he gets the job done with a no-hitter against the Indians in Cleveland. Jerry Browne flew out to right to end the game. On the same field, September, 24, 1988, he came close, only to see Julio Franco's two-out grounder to Manny Lee take a bad hop and bounce over his head and on into right field for a bad-hop single.

2. *Mike Flanagan vs. the Tigers October 3, 1987*
(12 innings, two runs, no decision)
Flanagan outduels Jack Morris, who left after nine innings on the second-last day of the regular season. From the fifth inning on manager Jimy Williams had a reliever warmed and ready to enter the game. Flanagan was one hit or a walk away from being removed. The Tigers could never manage the knock-out blow.

3. *Stieb vs. the Yankees August 4, 1989.*
(Nine innings, two hits, one run)
Stieb is an out away from a perfect game when Yankees outfielder Roberto Kelly lines a two-out double to left centre. Steve Sax follows with a run-scoring single, but Stieb escapes with a 2-1 win.

4. *Jim Clancy vs. the Twins, September 30, 1982.*
(Nine innings, one hit, zero runs)
Clancy retires the first 24 men in succession and takes his perfect game bid into the ninth. Randy Bush leads off for the Twins and shatters his bat as he swings. The ball flutters over the outstretched glove of second baseman Damaso Garcia. Clancy goes the rest of the way for a 3-0 victory.

5. *Jimmy Key vs. Tigers, June 6, 1985.*
(10 innings, two hits, zero runs)
Key took a no-hit bid into the ninth. Tom Brookens leads off with a single to left field. The Jays eventually win 2-0 on a Buck Martinez homer.

Four pitchers you'd least like to see on the mound with the bases loaded
1. *Joey McLaughlin*
22-24, 3.88, 31 saves, 343 hits and 148 walks in 341 innings.
2. *Roy Lee Jackson*
24-21, 3.50, 30 saves, 307 hits, 128 walks in 337 innings.
3. *Jerry Garvin*
20-41, 4.46, 648 hits and 219 walks in 606 innings, allowed three grand slam homers.
4. *Jeff Byrd*
2-13, 6.18, 98 hits and 68 walks in 87 1/3 innings.

Five biggest homers
1. *Ed Sprague off Atlanta's Jeff Reardon, October 18, 1992.*
Jays trail the Braves 2-1 entering the top of the ninth and are three outs away from being down 2-0 in the World Series. Derek Bell walks and pinch hitter Sprague hits a two-run homer to give the Jays the victory.
2. *George Bell off Bobby Thigpen of the White Sox, May 28, 1989.*
In the 10th inning of the final game at Exhibition Stadium, the score is tied. Kelly Gruber leads off with a double and Bell follows with a two-run homer into the left-field seats, bringing down the curtain on Exhibition Stadium.
3. *Candy Maldonado off Oakland's Mike Moore, October 13, 1992.*
Maldonado hits a three-run homer to put the Jays on their way to a lopsided win over Oakland.
4. *Willie Upshaw off Joe Cowley, October 5, 1985.*
His drive to right field put the Jays up 3-0 and that was all Doyle Alexander needed on the way a 5-1 victory over the Yankees, on the second-last day of the season to wrap up the AL East, the first time the Jays had ever won anything.
5. *Junior Felix off Bob Stanley, June 2, 1989.*
Down 10-0 at one point, Felix hits a grand-slam, inside-the-park homer to spark the Jays to a come-from-behind win.

Five best trades

1. Acquired 2B Robbie Alomar and OF Joe Carter from the Padres for 1B Fred McGriff and SS Tony Fernandez, December 5, 1990, at the winter meetings in Chicago.

Fernandez was moved after his second season with the Padres, traded to the Mets, while McGriff remains one of the biggest home run threats in the NL. In two seasons Alomar has a .302 average with 17 homers, 145 RBIs and 102 steals, while Carter owns a .268 batting average, with 77 homers and 227 RBIs. Both are tied up in long-term contracts.

2. Acquired RP Duane Ward from the Braves for RHP Doyle Alexander July 5, 1986.

Ward is now the stopper and has appeared in 377 games — third highest in club history, while going 30-32 with a 3.20 ERA, 76 saves and 571 strikeouts in 576-1/3 innings. Alexander didn't do much in Atlanta, but helped the Tigers win the AL East in '87.

3. Acquired OF Dave Collins, RHP Mike Morgan and 1B Fred McGriff from the Yankees for RP Dale Murray, December 9 1982, at the winter meetings in Hawaii.

Collins was a solid contributor, batting .291 the next two seasons, hitting .308 in 1984 with a two-year total of three homers, 78 RBIs and 91 steals; Morgan was winless in 16 games before being drafted by Seattle; McGriff batted .278, hit 125 homers and drove in 305 runs in four years and enabled the Jays to make the deal with San Diego for Robbie Alomar and Joe Carter. Meanwhile Murray had one save in 63 games over the next three seasons.

4. Acquired Juan Guzman for Mike Sharperson from the Dodgers, September 22, 1987.

Sharperson has been an effective back-up for the Dodgers and reached all-star status in 1992, but in 51 starts Guzman is 26-8 with a 2.79 ERA.

5. Acquired CF Devon White, RP Willie Fraser and RHP Marcus Moore from the Angels for OF Junior Felix, INF Luis Sojo and C Ken Rivers December 2, 1990.

Fraser was a bust and Moore went to the Rockies in the expansion draft while Felix was selected by the Marlins. White, however, solved a gigantic hole in centre field for the

Blue Jays. In two years he's hit a combined .265 with 34 homers, 120 RBIs and 70 steals.

Five worst deals
1. *Acquired RHP Mark Lemongello, OF J.J. Cannon and INF Pedro Hernandez from the Astros for C Alan Ashby, November 27, 1978.*

With the Jays, Lemongello was demoted during his first season after going 1-9 with a 6.29 ERA, Cannon batted .171 in parts of two seasons and Hernandez was hitless in nine at bats with the Jays. Ashby, meanwhile, played 11 years for Houston appearing in 965 games and helping the Astros to two NL West division titles.

2. *Cecil Fielder's contract sold to the Hanshin (Japan) Tigers.*

Fielder returned to sign as a free-agent with the Detroit Tigers and has been knocking down fences ever since.

3. *Acquired RHP Tommy Underwood and RP Victor Cruz from St. Louis for RHP Pete Vuckovich and OF John Scott.*

Vuckovich later won the Cy Young award, while Underwood was a combined 15-30, 3.88, and Cruz was 7-3 with a 1.71 ERA and nine saves in his only season.

4. *Acquired RP Bill Caudill from Oakland for OF Dave Collins and SS Alfredo Griffin.*

Caudill was the supposed messiah as a bullpen closer. He held the job until the end of July 1985 when Tom Henke was recalled from Syracuse. In two seasons he was 6-10 with a not-so-real-fine ERA of 4.09, while saving 16 games.

5. *Acquired RP Bryan Clark from the Mariners for OF Barry Bonnell.*

Clark wasn't the left-handed relief help the Jays were looking for as he was 1-2 with a 5.91 ERA in 24 games. While Bonnell, coming off a .318 season, hit only .253 in his two-plus seasons with Seattle, Clark was a bigger disappointment.

Six biggest snits
1. *DH George Bell.*

The reigning MVP stages a one-day sit-down strike St. Patrick's Day 1988 in Dunedin, refusing to DH against the Red Sox to protest his move from left field.

2. *David Wells.*

Late in the '91 season, Cito Gaston and Wells have a strong disagreement over pitch selection. Wells refuses to call the pitch Gaston wants and Mike Greenwell hits a two-run single. Gaston stomps to the mound yelling at Wells, who quickly leaves the mound and fires the ball into foul territory down the left field line. Fans boo Wells as he leaves the mound and cheer Gaston.

3. *Damaso Garcia.*

With the score tied 3-3 in the sixth on May 14, 1986 at Oakland, Garcia misplays a ball off the bat of Ricky Peters for an error and the A's go ahead against Dave Stieb. Stieb then gives up two homers. After the game Garcia burns his uniform in the showers.

4. *LF George Bell.*

Booed at SkyDome after a double hit by Bob Melvin of the Orioles falls out of his glove as he crashes into the left field fence, Bell rips the fans for booing him. He tells the press: "The fans can kiss my purple butt."

5. *SS Tony Fernandez.*

After striking out three times in his first three at bats against Brett Saberhagen in Kansas City, Fernandez heads up the tunnel to the clubhouse and doesn't return.

6. *LF George Bell.*

After being knocked down, Bell charges the mound early in the 1985 season to deliver a karate-chop kick to Boston right-hander Bruce Kison.

Five best Toronto baseball books
1. *CATCH: A Major League Life*
by Ernie Whitt and Greg Cable
2. *KELLY: At Home on Third*
by Kelly Gruber and Kevin Boland
3. *Second to None*
by Robbie Alomar and Stephen Brunt
4. *Baseball's Back in Town*
by Lou Cauz (history of the Triple-A Maple Leafs)
5. *Tomorrow I'll Be Perfect*
By Dave Stieb and Kevin Boland

All-time Team
C — *Ernie Whitt.* (Played 1,218 games, .253 batting avg. with 131 homers, 518 RBIs)
1B — *Fred McGriff.* (Played 578 games, .278 batting avg. with 125 homers, 305 RBIs)
2B — *Robbie Alomar.* (Played 313 games, .302 batting avg. with 17 homers, 145 RBIs and 102 steals)
3B — *Kelly Gruber.* (Played 921 games, .259 batting avg. with 114 homers, 434 RBIs.)
SS — *Tony Fernandez.* (Played 1,028 games, .289 batting avg., with 40 homers, 404 RBIs and 138 steals.)
LF — *George Bell.* (Played 1,181 games, .286 batting avg., with 202 homers, 740 RBIs.)
CF — *Devon White.* (Played 309 games, .265 batting avg. with 34 homers, 120 RBIs.)
RF — *Joe Carter.* (Played 320 games, .268 batting avg. with 77 homers and 227 RBIs.)
DH — *Dave Winfield.* (Played 156 games, .290 batting avg. with 26 homers and 108 RBIs.)
RHP — *Dave Stieb.* (Pitched 420 games, 174-132, 3.39 ERA.)
LHP — *Jimmy Key.* (Pitched 317 games, 116-81, 3.42 ERA.)
Reliever — *Tom Henke.* (Pitched 446 games, 29-29, 2.48 ERA, 217 saves.)

Dave Stieb never was perfect, but he came awfully close a number of times, and remains the best pitcher in Blue Jays history.
photo: Norm Betts/Toronto Sun

EXTRA INNINGS

◆1. Two men have worked as coaches for both the Montreal Expos and the Toronto Blue Jays. Who are they?

◆2. Not many Blue Jays developed colorful nicknames, but there have been a few. Identify the following players:
a) The Swatto
b) Shaker
c) The Inspector
d) Cuffs
e) Hogshead
f) Butch
g) The Terminator
h) Boomer
i) The Killer B's
j) Goose
k) Candy Man
l) The Beeg Mon
m) Thrill

◆3. They may be Canada's team, but only five Canadians have played for the Toronto Blue Jays. Name them.

◆4. Many great Blue Jay players hailed from San Pedro de Macoris in the Dominican Republic — Alfredo Griffin, George Bell, Damaso Garcia and Manny Lee among them. But who was the first?

♦5. During which season did the Jays first get permission to print World Series tickets?

♦6. What do Chris Chambliss, Aurelio Rodriguez and John Lowenstein have in common?

♦7. Who has played more seasons for the Blue Jays than any other?

♦8. During his playing days, this future Jays coach tied Babe Ruth's then-record of four World Series home runs and registered a record .913 slugging average in the '72 World Series. Who did it?

♦9. How many Cy Young Award winners have pitched for the Blue Jays?

♦10. Which Blue Jay, past or present, has hit the most major league home runs?

♦11. Which pitcher has started the most Opening Day games in Jays history?

♦12. Since the amateur free agent draft began in 1965, only 16 players have made it directly to the majors from amateur ball. Two of them made the jump to the Blue Jays — name them.

♦13. Before which season did the Blue Jays change their uniforms to a more traditional style?

♦14. Two Blue Jays have both played for and with Cito Gaston. Name them.

♦15. Which Blue Jay skipper was selected by the Expos as part of the 1968 Expansion Draft?

♦16. Name the three pitchers who pulled off no-hitters against the Jays.

◆17. This Blue Jay was the San Diego Padres' 30th and final selection in the 1968 expansion draft — name him.

◆18. Which three Blue Jays carried the middle names, respectively, of Lora, Lafayette and Caesar?

◆19. Name two Blue Jay pitchers who have credit for a pair of post-season victories *against* the Jays.

◆20. Which previous Blue Jays manager has Cito Gaston played for in the major leagues, and where?

◆21. Which Blue Jay set a major league record for highest fielding average at his position?

◆22. Which Blue Jay manager was chosen Manager of the Year by the Baseball Writers Association of America, UPI and AP?

◆23. Four pitchers in Jays' history share the record for most strikeouts in a game, with 12. Pete Vuckovich was the first, in 1977. Name the other three.

◆24. Who was the first Blue Jay player to be inducted to the Baseball Hall of Fame in Cooperstown?

◆25. Which Jay holds the all-time team record for appearances?

◆26. Name the future Blue Jay who hit the famous, game-winning single that dribbled through the legs of Bill Buckner, depriving the Red Sox of the World Series championship in 1986.

◆27. Which current Jays pitcher threw the earliest no-hitter in a season in AL history?

◆28. Which current Blue Jay has won four Gold Gloves in his career?

◆29. The Jays currently have the longest string of consecutive winning seasons with ten (1983-1992). How many more seasons will they have to play better than .500 to break the major league record?

◆30. Name the Blue Jay farmhand who was selected second over-all and first by the Florida Marlins in the 1993 expansion draft.

Answers begin on page 157.

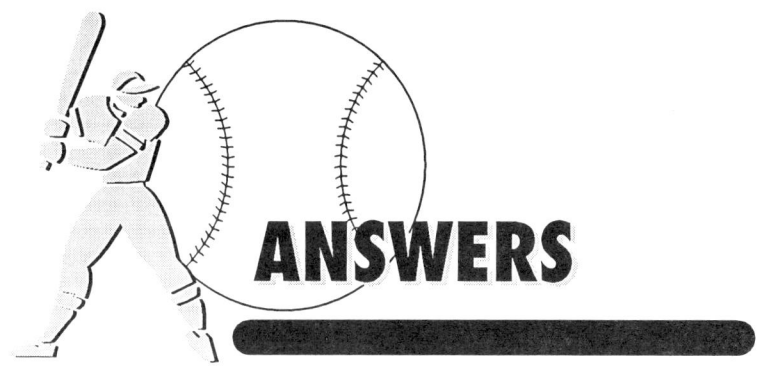

ANSWERS

FIRST INNING

1. The Seattle Mariners officially came into being on October 22, 1976. The Blue Jays followed on October 27.

2. The teams paid the princely sum of $175,000 for each player selected in the 1976 expansion draft.

3. Metro Baseball Limited was the short-term name of Toronto's expansion franchise.

4. The winner of the 'name the team' contest was selected by draw. The winner: 35-year-old periodontist Dr. William Mills. Dr. Mills received a trip for two to the Jays' first training camp and two season tickets, a prize package worth $2,000.

5. According to the *Times*, the Houston Astros were named as the team to trade places with the Blue Jays in the American League. The reason cited: to boost sagging attendance in Houston and in Arlington, Tex., with a Rangers-Astros AL rivalry touted as the answer. Meanwhile, the Expos could develop a rivalry with the Jays. The reputed switch wasn't to take place until 1978. Legendary sports writer Red Smith quickly denounced the rumor in his syndicated column: "For one thing, the Houston franchise has been a turkey ever since the nov-

That Magic Moment — the Blue Jays celebrate their World Series victory over Atlanta on October 25, 1992.

photo: Stan Behal/Toronto Sun

elty wore off the Astrodome, whereas Toronto looks like a winner at the box office." Besides, "the National League thinks it would contract a loathsome disease from close contact with the American Leaguers, and vice versa."

6. Pat Gillick was a pitcher. In fact, the southpaw pitched on the University of Southern California's 'World Series' championship team in 1958.

7. The bylaw prohibiting play on city property on Sundays had to be amended. Games were not to begin until after 1:30 p.m., to allow baseball fans time to go to church, pray for the early, dreadful Jays, and get to the ball game on time.

8. Hartsfield was an infielder for the Montreal Royals of the International League.

9. Miller was the first player signed by the Amazing Mets. Over the course of his 17-year big league career, Miller pitched for 10 clubs, tying a major league record.

10. Bobby Doerr was the Jays' first batting instructor.

11. Catcher Phil Roof, a 12-year major league veteran, was purchased from the Chicago White Sox on October 22, 1976. Because the team intended to use its choices in the upcoming expansion lottery to draft youth, they signed Roof for his leadership qualities and to steady a young pitching staff. As it turned out, Roof played only three games for the Jays, with five at-bats, and no hits.

12. In the 1976 draft, each existing AL team was allowed to protect 15 players. After a player was selected by an expansion team, they could add three more.

13. The Mariners selected OF Ruppert Jones from the Kansas City Royals.

14. Mark Belanger was the Orioles shortstop.

15. Jim Mason hit a home run for the Yankees in his only World Series at-bat.

16. Many scouts were concerned about the condition of Bailor's throwing arm, injured earlier that year in spring training. They believed reports of his arm problems would scare off the Jays and Mariners.

17. All these players were available to Seattle and Toronto in the 1976 expansion draft, but were not selected.

18. Alan Ashby. With the shortage of good catchers in the expansion draft, the Jays moved the 30-year-old KC pitcher to the Indians for Ashby.

19. In 1977, $30,000 would buy you an average Toronto Blue Jay for the season.

20. Early Wynn, who won 300 games over the course of his major league career, did color commentary on early Jays radio telecasts.

21. The Mariners felt it would be more difficult (and expensive) to sign a player if he knew he was selected in the early going. Toronto disagreed with the idea, and American League decided in their favor.

22. Rick Cerone was acquired from the Indians for Carty.

23. The Jays' first second baseman, Pedro Garcia, was second best AL rookie in 1973.

24. Jackie Moore, the Jays' original third base coach, was the Leafs' last skipper.

25. Ron Fairly was traded to the Expos in their debut season, 1969, for Maury Wills. On February 24, 1977, the A's traded Fairly to the Jays for infielder Mike Weathers.

26. Dave Lemancyk, the Jays' leading game winner in 1977, pitched Ontario Inter-County ball.

27. Bobby Cox played third base for the Yankees.

28. Jays coach Don Leppert (1977-79) was one of nine Yankees sent to the Baltimore Orioles in exchange for eight players in 1954, a 17-player swap. This was the trade, incidentally, which brought Don Larsen, who would later throw the only no-hitter in World Series history, to the Yankees.

SECOND INNING

1. The Jays beat the Mets 3-1 in their first spring training game.

2. Right-handed pitcher Steve Hargan was the first Jay to hold out for more money. After an agreement was reached, he promptly got injured, then made only six appearances before becoming this trivia question.

3. Dave McKay, the Blue Jays' first Canadian player, made this startling discovery. Better late than never.

4. Robin Godfrey, the son of then-Metro Toronto Chairman Paul Godfrey.

5. Tim Nordbrook would join the Jays later that season, while Jorge Orta would DH for the Jays in 1983.

6. Nope — they lost 3-2 to the White Sox, with Dave McKay grounding into a double play in the bottom of the ninth, with runners on first and third.

7. DH Otto Velez was selected AL Player of the Month for April 1977.

8. Chuck Hartenstein, nicknamed "Twiggy," pitched only 27.1 innings for the '77 Blue Jays, junk pitches and all.

9. Doug Ault, Opening Day's hero, threw left-handed but batted right exclusively.

10. Roy Howell had a career afternoon at the ball park on September 10, 1977.

11. Jerry Johnson became a stunt man in Hollywood, and his TV credits include *Little House on the Prairie* and *Hawaii 5-0*.

12. Luis Gomez was the first player signed in the re-entry draft in 1977.

13. Shortstop Bob Bailor, 1B Doug Ault and LHP Jerry Garvin were all selected to the 1977 all-rookie team.

14. Sam Ewing batted .287 for the '77 Blue Jays and even had his own fan club. But his average fell to .179 in 1978 and he was gone.

15. Steve Staggs, who shared second base duties with Pedro Garcia, took a walk after the Jays refused to give him a raise. "My feeling is if the Dodgers could survive the retirement of Sandy Koufax, we'll have to get along without Steve," team president Peter Bavasi told the press. "We lost 107 games on the field. Some players didn't earn lasting wealth."

16. Lemancyk's 13th win of the season tied him with Gene Brabender of the '69 Seattle Pilots for most wins by a pitcher on a first-year expansion team. Mind you, Lemancyk's 20 wild pitches was one shy of the American League record set by Walter Johnson of the Washington Senators in 1910.

17. Phil Roof announced his retirement after the Jays final game of the '77 campaign, while pitcher Bill Singer, who had back surgery in the off season, followed later.

18. Lyman Bostock was the Jays first free agent selection.

19. Ron Fairly became the first player since Stan the Man to play more than 1000 games in both the infield and outfield.

20. Bob Bailor's .310 batting average was best ever for an expansion team.

21. Jerry Garvin led the AL in '77 with 22 pickoffs.

22. Manager Roy Hartsfield spun this downhome analysis of his '77 Jays.

THIRD INNING

1. Victor Cruz boasted a sparkling 1.71 ERA with a 7-3 record and nine saves in 1978.

2. Catcher Brian Milner made his debut in that game. The 18-year-old, considered to be the Jays catcher of the future, got three hits. Ironically, he played only one other game with the Jays.

3. Rico Carty was originally obtained from the Cleveland Indians in the '76 *expansion draft*, and was subsequently traded back to the Indians (for Alan Ashby and Doug Howard). The Jays *traded* for Carty in '78, giving up pitcher Dennis DeBarr, before trading him away again later that year to the Oakland A's for Willie Horton and Phil Huffman. Finally, they signed him as a *free agent* in January 1979.

4. He was the toughest to strike out — seeing a third strike only 21 times in 621 at-bats in 1978.

5. Balor Moore.

6. Eichhorn, the Cabrillo Jr. College star, was listed as a shortstop in the draft. (Dave Stieb, drafted six months earlier, was an outfielder.)

7. John Castino of the Minnesota Twins was co-winner of

the AL Rookie of the Year award.

8. Rick Bosetti became the first Blue Jay to play all 162 regular season games.

9. The worst third year team in modern history was the '63 New York Mets, with a 53-109 mark — a record they now share with the '79 Jays.

10. Pitchers Jerry Garvin, in 1977, and Phil Huffman, in '79, each lost 18 games.

11. Jay Schroeder went on to quarterback the Washington Redskins and the L.A. Raiders — but he gave baseball his best shot. He toiled for the Jays in their minor league system, but hit a modest .213 and struck out 477 times in four seasons.

12. Peter Bavasi. On behalf of the players, Roy Howell retorted: "How do you think our wives feel about that remark?"

13. The 1899 Cleveland Spiders finished 12th in the National League, 36 games behind 11th place Washington and a whopping *80* behind first place Brooklyn, with a 20-134 record.

14. The Jays bullpen notched only 11 saves in 1979, one fewer than the previous worst mark. By way of comparison, the Cubs' Bruce Sutter got 37 all by himself in 1979.

15. Steve Luebber's ERA: infinity. He gave up two doubles and a walk to the Red Sox without getting anybody out before he was lifted.

16. In 1979, Alfredo Griffin was charged with a record 37 errors. The Blue Jay brain trust professed not to care, saying the mark was so high because he got to balls most other shortstops generally miss.

17. The Pearson Cup, named for former prime minister Lester B. Pearson, was the annual exhibition between the Jays and Expos. Unfortunately, fan interest in the game was low and the game was regularly derided by the participants as a waste of a perfectly good off-day.

18. In 1936, while playing in the minors, he suffered a serious eye injury when he was struck by a foul ball while standing by a batting cage. The resulting double vision hampered his career, although he did get to the bigs, playing for the Cubs and the Reds before retiring in 1942.

19. Mattick allowed the players to wear their hair and moustaches as they pleased, and lifted the ban against players drinking in the hotels they stayed in on the road.

20. The Senators set a record for most consecutive 100 or more games lost in consecutive seasons with four, between 1961 and 1964. The much-improved 1980 Jays lost 95 after three consecutive 100+ loss seasons.

21. Roy Howell's departure left an opening at 3B that was difficult to fill. Although Howell hit .269 in 1980 with 10 game winning RBIs, his 16 errors disappointed. The team figured Ainge would provide better defence.

22. George Bell sat out most of the 1980 season with a pinched back muscle, and the Phillies assumed that teams would steer clear of him. They also hid him on a Dominican Republic B Team once he recovered. But Jays senior scout Al Lamacchia located Bell, scouted him without being spotted by team officials, and recommended the Jays select him in the draft.

23. Roy Lee Jackson.

24. Ainge received a $300,000 bonus "not to engage in or play professional basketball," a sum he had to repay.

FOURTH INNING

1. Buck Martinez was acquired before the '81 season to platoon at catcher with Ernie Whitt. Martinez was an original member of the Kansas City Royals in 1969.
2. Len Barker sent 27 Jays down in order on that afternoon in Cleveland.
3. Ainge won the John Wooden Award as the U.S. College Basketball Player of the Year.
4. Big John Mayberry's 1981 payday put him at the top of the list — for a short time.
5. Stieb was the first Jays' regular starter to win more decisions than he lost.
6. Ainge was a second round draft choice of the Boston Celtics in the 1981 NBA draft.
7. The Jays signed Dong Won Choi, a right-handed pitcher, the first South Korean inked by a major league team. Unfortunately, he never came to Canada, saying he wanted a guarantee he could play for the major league team right away.
8. Cito Gaston became the Jays' first full-time batting instructor.
9. No one. Peter Hardy became CEO of the Jays the following year, representing the team at league meetings, while Pat Gillick and Paul Beeston continued to manage player personnel and business operations, respectively. The Jays were without a president until Beeston got the appointment on January 10, 1989.
10. Each of them grounded into the only triple plays in Jays' history. Junior Moore did it while playing for the White Sox on April 22, 1978; Cox did the favor while he was a Cleveland Indian in 1979, and Garcia made it easier for

the Yankees to trade him to the Jays when he touched off the third and final triple play in Jays' history, on September 21, 1979.

11. Willie Upshaw, more mobile and putting up creditable offensive numbers of his own, took away Mayberry's job at first base.

12. Jerry Garvin became a free agent at the end of the '82 season, tried and failed to hook-up with the St. Louis Cardinals, before being reacquired by the Jays during spring training the following year. He was assigned to Syracuse, but never returned to the big club.

13. The Royals traded Cecil Fielder to the Jays for Leon Roberts.

14. The Jays' double play combo of Alfredo Griffin and Damaso Garcia.

15. Hosken Powell.

16. Fred McGriff came to Toronto in the Collins trade.

17. Tippy Martinez came into the game with an inherited runner on first base, Barry Bonnell. He promptly picked him off. He then walked Dave Collins — and picked him off. Then Willie Upshaw singled and, before he knew it, he was picked off too. The inning summed up the Jays' luck during the last week of August '83, when they lost six games in a row in the final inning, four of them in extra innings.

18. Cliff Johnson and Jorge Orta made up the most effective DH corps in the AL in '83.

19. Dave Collins was an original member of the Mariners.

20. Rance Mulliniks led all AL third basemen in fielding percentage from 1984 to 1986.

FIFTH INNING

1. Aikens had been sentenced to three months imprisonment for attempting to possess cocaine, and was in jail through most of spring training. He also also under suspension by the league, which was not lifted until May.

2. Rick Leach starred as quarterback for the Michigan Wolverines in his college days.

3. Rick Leach, the last non-pitcher to take the mound in Jays' history, went in to mop up a game against the Indians. Trailing 14-1 to the Indians in the top of a doubleheader, the Jays sent Leach to the hill after he told Cox he used to pitch in high school. He gave up three runs on two hits and walked two, the least successful of the three non-pitchers to do the job in Jays' history.

4. Dave Collins swiped 60 bases in 1984.

5. Manuel Lee and Lou Thornton were picked up from the Astros and Mets respectively, and both were playing at the A ball level at the time. While both made contributions to the Jays' AL East pennant drive, some would argue that hanging on to these "not-ready-for-prime-time" players hurt the Jays in the long run.

6. Joey McLaughlin wore number 50 before Tom Henke rehabilitated it.

7. When Cliff Johnson signed with the Texas Rangers as a free agent after the '84 season, the Jays got Henke in the compensation draft. (Johnson was traded back to the Jays the following season for three minor leaguers.)

8. Caudill's 14 saves in '85 broke Dale Murray's then-record seasonal save mark of 12. Henke, who got 13 the same year, would later set the current team mark of 34.

9. The New York Yankees picked up most of Alexander's

salary during his tenure with the Jays — another reason George Steinbrenner belongs in the Canadian Baseball Hall of Fame!

10. Oliver wore '0'

11. On August 6 and 7, the players staged a two-day walk-out. Once back to work, the Jays made up one of the two postponed games in a doubleheader and slated the other to be played after the season ended, if necessary.

12. Yankees catcher Ron Hassey launched it at 4:28 p.m. for the final out in the clinching game.

13. Phil Niekro got win number 300 on October 6, 1985 in a nothing game for the Jays.

14. Team physician Dr. Ron Taylor pitched for the Amazing Mets of '69.

15. The "X Factor" had to do with the number of former Chicago Cubs on a team's roster going into a playoff. Over the 40 years between the Cubs' last World Series and 1985, teams with three or more ex-Cubs had lost post-season series 92 per cent of the time. The Jays were cursed with four: Dennis Lamp, Cliff Johnson, Bill Caudill and Tom Filer. The Royals had none. (The other division champions, the Dodgers and the Cards, had two apiece.)

16. Jeff Hearron appeared in Games 4 and 6 of the '85 ALCS.

17. Royals' catcher Jim Sundberg's wind-assisted triple drove in three runs in the sixth inning and ended the Jays' pennant hopes.

18. Pitcher Bill Caudill was the only Jay not to see any action during the 1985 ALCS.

19. George Brett drove Jays fans bonkers with his timely

hitting in the 1985 ALCS.

20. The league championship series for both leagues were best of five affairs until the 1985 season when they became best of seven. The Jays led the '85 series three games to one after the fourth game.

SIXTH INNING

1. Ron Fairly was Toronto's token contribution to the AL squad in 1977.

2. Dave Lemancyk was Toronto's token contribution to the AL All-Star team in 1979.

3. Third baseman Roy Howell was the Jays' sole All-Star representative in the team's second season, 1978.

4. Early Wynn, who shared the broadcast booth with Tom Cheek at early Jays games, also made seven All-Star appearances.

5. Stieb threw two wild pitches, tying the All-star Game and inning record with Marichal.

6. Damaso Garcia hit a leadoff single in the eighth inning of the 1985 All-Star Game.

7. George Bell was the first Jay to make the All-Star team by ballot.

8. Dave Stieb made his first plate appearance in the 1981 All-Star Game in Cleveland, when he struck out in the ninth. Two years later in Chicago, Stieb's sacrifice bunt set up an unearned run for the American League.

9. Catcher Gary Carter put one in the stands at Candlestick Park against Sir Dave, in one of the few Expo-Blue Jay confrontations at the mid-season classic.

10. In 1989, Kelly Gruber tied Mays' record for steals in an All-Star game with two. He pulled off the first as a pinch-runner for Wade Boggs, then, after walking in the next inning, scooped another.

11. False — Montreal hosted the game in 1983.

12. Jimmy Key was the pitcher of record in the AL's 1991 victory.

13. Tom Henke sported a 0-2 won-loss record going into the 1987 All-Star Game.

14. Fred McGriff.

SEVENTH INNING

1. Williams owned and operated a grocery store in St. Louis in 1972 and '73.

2. Unruly fans kept running out on the field causing delays. In all 126 fans were ejected and 45 were arrested, mostly on alcohol-related charges. In addition, three policemen were hurt.

3. Damaso Garcia, days after setting fire to his uniform in the Jays locker room to protest his treatment by the team, appeared in the fire safety promotion.

4. Jesse Barfield's 40 homers in 1986 was the best in the majors.

5. Outfielder Jesse Barfield and shortstop Tony Fernandez were the first Jays to win Rawlings Gold Glove awards, recognizing fielding excellence.

6. Tony Fernandez's record indicates he showed up for work 163 times in 1986.

7. Tom Quinlan, unlike Jay Schroeder and Danny Ainge

before him, decided to stick with baseball.

8. In 1986, Tony Fernandez's 213 hits set the new standard for shortstops.

9. Dave Stieb led the AL in 1986 with a 2.48 ERA.

10. Jim Clancy got win number 100 on July 28, 1986.

11. That was the year the Jays kicked off their season 90 minutes before the Cincinnati Reds' opening pitch. Traditionally the Reds, the oldest team in major league baseball, got the honor of starting first. The Jays explained they were starting early to avoid the same drunken scene they'd had the year before. It was also the first time that the baseball season was starting outside of the U.S., which irked American fans.

12. Phil Niekro and Steve Carlton combined to beat the Jays that day. Niekro got the win with Carlton coming on in relief, picking up just his second career save, and his first since 1968. The pitchers had 42 years of experience between them!

13. The Orioles returned to their orange jerseys after a four-year absence.

14. The 48-year-old knuckleballer and 24-year major league veteran had never been traded before. The Jays sent minor league outfielder Daryl Landrum to the Indians for Niekro.

15. On September 14, 1987, the Blue Jays hammered 10 home runs against the Orioles, shattering the old major-league record of eight in a game. Bats belonging to Whitt, who broke the old mark, and McGriff, who set the new one, were sent to Cooperstown.

16. Orlando (Cha Cha) Cepeda.

17. The Jays sold Upshaw to the Cleveland Indians during spring training in 1988.

18. It was the reason cited for the explosion of home runs recorded in 1987, the year the Jays led the league in homers with 215, sixth highest ever for a major league team. In 1987, 4,458 home runs were hit in major league baseball, shattering the old mark of 3,813 by a wide margin. Why the sudden jump? Many speculated it was the result of using a different kind of glue in the manufacture of official balls, making the surface harder. Former Major League pitcher Claude Osteen thought the balls were different because the baseball cover was cut fractionally smaller, meaning the seam bound more tightly, producing a taut surface with low seams. Whatever the reason, home run totals everywhere plunged the following year — the Jays hit only 158 in 1988.

19. Tom Henke made a league record 72 appearances without a win to his credit in the '87 season. At the same time, he notched a team-record 34 saves with a 2.49 ERA.

20. Fred McGriff's 20 homers in 1987 is the team's rookie standard.

EIGHTH INNING

1. He didn't pull any — in fact, 1988 was the only year in team history that the Jays did not swing a trade. It was in the midst of Pat Gillick's famed 608-day "Stand Pat" trade interim, which ended when he traded Jesse Barfield to the Yankees for pitcher Al Leiter in April 1989.

2. George Bell became the first major leaguer to hit three home runs on Opening Day.

3. It was the longest nine-inning game in team history, at four hours and 15 minutes. There was plenty to see — six unearned runs, three errors, three batters hit by

pitches, two wild pitches, two balks, a passed ball, 32 hits, 23 runners left on base and 399 pitches to 89 batters. The Jays won 17-9.

4. No — the Yankees' Whitey Ford did it in 1955, and Sam McDowell was similarly snakebit in 1966.

5. Julio Franco of the Indians spoiled Stieb's no-hit bid, while the Orioles' Jim Traber did the disfavor the following game. Almost a year later, it was the Yankees' Roberto Kelly's turn in Stieb's third no-hit bid.

6. b) 15 — it just *seemed* like more!

7. David Wells won a pair from the Angels that day.

8. It was Bob Brenly, when he played for the Giants. But the story has a happy ending — he drove in five runs the same game, including a ninth-inning homer to win the game.

9. Third baseman Kelly Gruber is the only Jay to hit for cycle, in this order: HR, double, triple then single.

10. Nelson Liriano ruined Nolan Ryan's day, on April 23, 1989, when he hit a triple to break up his no-hit bid in the ninth. And on April 28, California's Kirk McCaskill had to settle for a one-hitter when Liriano doubled off him.

11. Frank Robinson, Maury Wills and Larry Doby preceded Gaston.

12. Cito's real name is Clarence Edwin Gaston. His pals started calling him 'Cito' after a Mexican wrestler. "I never knew anything about the guy," Gaston says, "but if your given name is Clarence, you take any nickname you can get."

13. Mookie was born William Hayward Wilson.

14. Hitting a home run, first time up to bat, on the first pitch.

15. Junior Felix was the first player to hit an inside-the-ball park grand slam in 24 years.

16. Yes. After 968 games at the Ex, the Jays posted a 491-475 record.

17. Chuck Hartenstein was a member of the Jays' pitching staff on Opening Day 1977, and the Milwaukee Brewers' pitching coach when the Jays played their first game at SkyDome.

18. Paul Molitor was the first man at the plate at the Dome opener. He hit a double.

19. After the stadium was built, it was discovered that regulation foul poles would be difficult to install because of the parking lot built directly below the field. So foul chains are lowered from the ceiling and are hooked up at field level.

20. The Jays were a perfect 11-0 at SkyDome in '89 with the roof closed during the regular season.

21. Tom Lawless was traded from the Cincinnati Reds to the Montreal Expos for Pete Rose, straight-up, on August 16, 1984.

22. Lee Mazzilli was picked up from the Mets on waivers.

23. That was Jays outfielder Mookie Wilson hanging out with Cookie Monster, Big Bird and Oscar the Grouch.

24. In a game against the Brewers in Milwaukee, Tony Fernandez was in the on-deck circle in the fifth when Ernie Whitt grounded out to end the inning. In the top of the sixth, he was on the bench as Gruber went to the plate. Gruber flied out, but would have been out if he

had reached base anyway.

25. Rickey Henderson swiped an LCS record eight bases in the five-game Oakland A's series victory of the Jays in 1989.

NINTH INNING

1. Joe Carter holds the distinction of being the first man to have three consecutive 100 RBI seasons with three different teams.

2. Pat Borders.

3. In 1991, the Jays were the "swing team," finishing their schedule against West Division opponents, and became the first such team to win a divisional crown since divisional play began in 1969.

4. Rick Cerone appeared in 136 games as catcher in 1979.

5. It was the 13th season in a row that Morris was Opening Day pitcher, an AL record.

6. Jose Pett became Brazil's first pro baseball player in '92.

7. John Smoltz narrowly captured the NL strikeout title from Cone.

8. They coughed up an AL record 31 hits to the Brewers, breaking the old record of 30, and tied the major league mark set by the New York Giants in 1901.

9. The Jays were five runs behind, trailing 6-1, before they began their comeback, on their way to a 7-6 victory.

10. Roberto Alomar, with his .423 ALCS average and numerous clutch hits, was chosen MVP.

11. Francisco Cabrera.

12. Morris, the first pitcher in Jays' history to win 20 games in a season, went 0-3 in four starts during the 1992 ALCS/World Series.

13. Ed Sprague, whose two-run homer in the ninth-inning of Game 2 gave the Jays a come-from-behind victory.

14. A lot of Jay-watchers will tell you Kelly Gruber placed a diving tag on Deion Sanders before he got back to second base.

15. Lonnie Smith's fifth-inning grand slam, the first by a National Leaguer in 18 years of World Series play, effectively sent the series back to Atlanta for Game 6.

16. None, tying a record.

17. Most games batted safely in a post-season by a catcher, with 14. The old record, 11, was shared by Thurman Thomas and Yogi Berra.

18. Joe Carter started at left field, right field and first base during the '92 Series, to tie the record for most positions started.

19. Dave Winfield's 0-22 drought in 1981 tied him with Dal Maxvilli for worst post-season streak — until Kelly came along.

20. Jimmy Key, in his last appearance as a Jay, picked up the win.

EXTRA INNINGS

1. Galen Cisco and Jackie Moore have worked for both of Canada's major league teams.

2. a) Otto Velez
   b) Lloyd Moseby
   c) Bill Caudill
   d) Bill Caudill

e) Roy Howell
f) Claude Edge (early Jays pitcher)
g) Tom Henke
h) Believe it or not, the Jays had *two* Boomer Wells; Greg Wells, a 1B-DH in 1981, and current pitcher David Wells.
i) George Bell and Jesse Barfield
j) Mauro Gozzo
k) Candy Maldonado
l) Rico Carty
m) Glenallen Hill

3. *Dave McKay* of Vancouver, B.C. was an original Blue Jay, playing third base in the first game. *Paul Hodgson*, from Fredericton, N.B., played outfield for the Jays in 1980. *Rob Ducey* was the third Canadian Jay, and the first Toronto-native, making outfield appearances from 1987 to 1991. In 1991, pitcher *Denis Boucher* of Lachine, P.Q. made his debut with the Jays, as did lefty *Vince Horsman* of Dartmouth, N.S.

4. Rico Carty was the first Jay to hail from San Pedro de Macoris.

5. On September 21, 1981, the Jays were granted permission to print World Series. Owing to the split-season set-up, and the fact they were only 3-1/2 games behind for the second half AL East championship, they got the nod.

6. Each were traded to the Jays, but were traded away again before they played an official game for the team.

7. That would be pitcher Dave Stieb, who left the Jays after the '92 season to try his luck with the Chicago White Sox. Stieb played 14 seasons for the Jays. Next best are Jim Clancy and Ernie Whitt at 12.

8. Gene Tenace.

9. Two — Pete Vuckovich, an original Jay, won the Cy Young with the Brewers in 1982. Mike Flanagan, a Blue

Jay from 1987 to '89, won the Cy Young in 1979 while he was a Baltimore Oriole.

10. Entering the '93 season, Dave Winfield has hit 432 homers over his illustrious career, 20th place on the all-time list.

11. Dave Stieb's four Opening Day starts (1983, '85, '86 and '91) lead the team. Jimmy Key is second with three (1987 through '89).

12. Catcher Brian Milner made the jump directly to the Jays in 1978; first baseman John Olerud did it in 1989.

13. The current uniforms, with traditional button-down fronts, and road greys replacing powder blue, hit the diamond in 1989.

14. In 1990, pitcher John Candelaria became the first player to have played both for and with the Jays' manager. Candelaria was a member of the Pittsburgh Pirate staff when Gaston was traded to the team in September 1978, at the end of Gaston's playing career. In 1992, Dave Winfield played for Gaston — he broke into the majors with the San Diego Padres in 1973, Gaston's fifth year with the Pods.

15. Jimy Williams was selected by Montreal in 1968, but never made the big club.

16. Len Barker (Indians, 1981 — perfect game), Dave Stewart (A's, 1990) and Nolan Ryan (Texas, 1991) have all no-noed the Jays.

17. Manager Cito Gaston was last chosen by the Pods in the '68 draft.

18. Manuel Lee, Doyle Alexander and Tom Candiotti.

19. Dave Stewart won games one and five of the 1989 ALCS for the A's, while Jack Morris broke our hearts twice

during the '91 ALCS while with the Twins.

20. Gaston played for Bobby Cox's Atlanta Braves in 1978.

21. Tony Fernandez' .992 fielding average at shortstop in 1987 is the standard for the position.

22. Bobby Cox got the triple nod in 1985.

23. Jim Clancy (1988), Dave Stieb (1988) and Tom Candiotti (1991) were the other Jay pitchers to strike out 12 in the same game.

24. Jimmy Foxx. Okay, so it's a trick question. But for a brief period during the '40s, the National League's Philadelphia Phillies were known as the Blue Jays, and Foxx, number nine on the all-time list of home run hitters, played for them in 1945. While we're at it, can you name the only Canadian pitcher to ever win a game for the Blue Jays? That would be Ingersoll, Ontario's Oscar Judd, who was 5-4 with the '45 Blue Jays.

25. "The Shaker," Lloyd Moseby, played in a team record 1392 games.

26. Mookie Wilson gave Red Sox fans heart failure when Buckner misplayed his weak hit in the '86 World Series.

27. Jack Morris pitched a no-hitter against the White Sox on April 7, 1984 while employed by the Tigers.

28. Centre fielder Devon White won Gold Gloves in 1988, '89, '91 and '92.

29. Would you believe *30* more seasons? The New York Yankees' 39-year streak (1926-1964) is the major league record so far, but the Jays should be able to set the new mark in the year 2023 — if Duane Ward's arm holds out!

30. Canada's own Nigel Wilson.